CU00542926

Penguin Monarchs

THE HOUSE OF TUDOR

Henry VII	Sean Cunningham
Henry VIII*	John Guy
Edward VI*	Stephen Alford
Mary I*	John Edwards
Elizabeth I	Helen Castor

THE HOUSE OF STUART

James I	Thomas Cogswell
Charles I*	Mark Kishlansky
[Cromwell*	David Horspool]
Charles II*	Clare Jackson
James II	David Womersley
William III & Mary II*	Jonathan Keates
Anne	Richard Hewlings

THE HOUSE OF HANOVER

George I	Tim Blanning
George II	Norman Davies
George III	Jeremy Black
George IV	Stella Tillyard
William IV	Roger Knight
Victoria*	Jane Ridley

THE HOUSES OF SAXE-COBURG & GOTHA AND WINDSOR

Edward VII*	Richard Davenport-Hines
George V*	David Cannadine
Edward VIII*	Piers Brendon
George VI*	Philip Ziegler
Elizabeth II*	Douglas Hurd

* Now in paperback

DAVID WOODMAN

Edward the Confessor
The Sainted King

ALLEN LANE
an imprint of
PENGUIN BOOKS

ALLEN LANE

UK | USA | Canada | Ireland | Australia
India | New Zealand | South Africa

Penguin Books is part of the Penguin Random House group of companies
whose addresses can be found at global.penguinrandomhouse.com

First published 2020
001

Copyright © David Woodman, 2020

The moral right of the author has been asserted

Set in 9.5/13.5 pt Sabon LT Std
Typeset by Jouve (UK), Milton Keynes
Printed and bound in Great Britain by Clays Ltd, Elcograf S.p.A.

ISBN: 978-0-241-38300-1

www.greenpenguin.co.uk

Contents

For Sasha,
who is simply perfect

Introduction

On 7 February 1161, Pope Alexander III issued a papal bull – a form of public decree – which bestowed sainthood on Edward, the king who ruled in England between 1042 and 1066. From this moment Edward was admitted to the ranks of the holy confessors (those saints who died of natural causes) from where he derives his honorific 'the Confessor'. This is how Edward is best known to us: as a royal saint who lies buried in Westminster Abbey. But this is the Edward of myth, not the Edward of history. The majority of this book is concerned with the eleventh-century Edward, before we survey (in Chapter 5) his 'afterlife', the circumstances in which he was canonized and the ways in which he remained an important national figure into the thirteenth century.

The Edward of the mid to late eleventh century is accessible to us in various ways. A number of near-contemporary sources have fortunately been preserved. These range from narrative texts about Edward's mother (the *Encomium Emmae Reginae*) or (nominally) about Edward himself (the *Vita Ædwardi Regis*) to documentary evidence such as royal diplomas and writs, to material evidence such as coins, royal seals and the Bayeux Tapestry. There were also Anglo-Norman texts (such as William of Malmesbury's *Gesta Regum Anglorum* and John of Worcester's *Chronicle*): Norman historians were interested in Edward the Confessor's reign and we will meet two in particular, William of Jumièges and William of Poitiers. The surviving source material permits a relatively detailed depiction of the principal events of Edward's life: the authors of these texts were interested in royal action and in the major players at meetings of the Anglo-Saxon royal assembly (known as the witan). But it is imperative to understand that these same authors almost always have their own agendas and purpose. Those texts written after 1066, for example, seek in various ways to explain the events that led to the Norman conquest, and, in doing so, they quite often distort their accounts of Edward's reign in certain respects or omit material that does not suit their purpose. It is therefore vital for us to be aware of these added layers of complexity when trying to interpret the information contained in a particular text. Some of our sources provide details about Edward's physical characteristics and his temperament, but these are composed according to contemporary ideals of how kings should appear and with a certain purpose in mind; it is doubtful how far we can use such material to reconstruct Edward's real personality. But what emerges extremely clearly is the fraught and highly complex politics of those in the witan, with Edward at its head, from the mid eleventh century to his death in 1066.

The kingdom that we know as 'England' had only relatively recently come into being: its beginnings lay in the preceding century. It was ruled by a succession of kings from Wessex (in its origins an independent kingdom) who traced their descent back to a mythical founding figure called Cerdic. There was no strict rule of primogeniture, but those who became kings of the English in the eleventh

century before Edward (apart from those who reigned following military conquest) were members of this West Saxon
royal line; the Anglo-Saxon term used for a prince of royal
blood was 'ætheling'. Administratively speaking, England
of the eleventh century was very sophisticated. The kingdom was divided into a sequence of administrative districts,
known as shires, from which taxes (both in the form of
money and in kind) and military resources could be raised.
The king, via his royal agents (known as 'shire reeves', hence
'sheriffs'), had control over this network of districts and was
able to call on the finances raised and also on the services of
men as part of an army (known by the Old English term
fyrd) levied when needed, with the numbers of levied troops
calculated on the basis of the value of the land concerned
(which was measured in 'hides', where one hide was a vari-
able area equivalent to the amount of land needed to sustain
one family). Earls were important secular officials in the
kingdom who had control over their earldoms, which were
themselves territories composed of different and fluctuating
conglomerations of shires. Earls were powerful individuals
in the late Anglo-Saxon period and unprecedented levels of
influence were reached by Earl Godwine (who first became
earl in 1018, during the reign of King Cnut) and his sons;
Edward's relationship with this family – the 'Godwines' –
forms one of the principal themes of this book.

In his everyday administrative business, the king could
confirm grants of land in the form of the solemn royal diploma, or despatch mandates to local courts via the less
formal writ (which was authenticated by the use of a seal
attached to it).[1] He also attempted to keep order across

England by issuing new or confirming existing laws (no new laws survive from Edward's reign and those that travel under his name – the so-called *Leges Edwardi Confessoris* – are a Norman compilation). Such was the king's power in the mid eleventh century that the late Anglo-Saxon coinage is the only example in western Europe of the king enjoying a monopoly and being able to enforce regular recoinages and changes in style and design.[2]

The impressiveness of late Anglo-Saxon England and its system of government is undoubted. But if one looks beneath the surface, cracks can be seen. In fact, parts of the kingdom – notably the north of Northumbria – remained essentially separate, governed by their own series of important political figures. Rulership of England itself was, in the early eleventh century, on the eve of Edward's reign, ceded to Scandinavian kings of the fame of King Cnut and then his son Harthacnut. And, despite the administrative sophistication of the kingdom, there were serious logistical problems confronting Edward, for example in raising an army (which often took so long that he was obliged to disband any forces gathered) and in travelling across the kingdom (a network of Iron Age and Roman roads were used, as was a type of road known as an 'army path' – *herepæþ* (pronounced 'hare-a-path') in Old English – but journeys to the extremities of England took time; Edward himself rarely travelled beyond the heartlands of Wessex).[3] This made it all the harder for Edward to combat any threat of external invasion, a recurrent problem for all kings of the English in the eleventh century. In addition, trouble could be caused for Edward by those individuals who had been exiled from England, since the rulers of neighbouring kingdoms (in Britain and in Europe) offered places of refuge, where exiles could recover themselves and in time return to England to try to reclaim and even augment their former positions of power. It was imperative, therefore, for Edward to maintain his awareness of events and political alliances being made in north-western Europe and to establish his own network of allies.

There was a great deal for him to contend with, and, as we will see, our sources suggest (whether or not we can believe them) that he became frustrated at times. Edward also had to cope with natural disasters: during his reign, a contemporary text – the *Anglo-Saxon Chronicle* – refers to severe storms, the mass deaths of cattle, famine, even to an earthquake on 1 May 1048 that was felt in particular at Worcester, Droitwich and Derby; one season had been so harsh 'that there was no one alive who could remember so hard a winter as that was, both for pestilence and murrain, and birds and fish perished through the great cold and through hunger'.[4] There were also strong voices of discontent. The rule of Edward's immediate predecessor, Harthacnut, was remembered above all for its very high levels of taxation; people were to complain about these fiscal burdens into Edward's reign, a note of discord that influenced his own decisions about taxes. Again, the *Anglo-Saxon Chronicle* laments how, in 1044, the price of corn was 'dearer than anyone remembered'.[5]

This was the world with which Edward would become familiar: a kingdom that, although impressive in terms of its methods of government and centralized authority, nevertheless had problems of political fragmentation, and where wild oscillations in fortune regularly took place. Edward would experience these extreme fluctuations in his own life. Even if we are not permitted a view of Edward's real appearance or personality, we can trace the course of his life through the lens of contemporary sources, uncovering the complexities at the apex of society in eleventh-century England.

A Note on the
Anglo-Saxon Chronicle

The origins of the *Anglo-Saxon Chronicle* lie in the court of King Alfred the Great in the early 890s, to which additions were made at various subsequent stages in the Anglo-Saxon period and beyond. Information for Edward's reign is provided by three principal manuscript copies of the *Chronicle*, referred to by the letters C, D and E. For some entries these different versions contain broadly similar detail. For others (and this is particularly evident in their accounts of 1051–2) they exhibit stark differences that reflect the time in which they were written and the bias/interests of their authors. Versions C and E were seemingly written closer in time to the events they describe than D, which, in parts, may exhibit a post-1066 perspective. Arguments have been made that C was composed at various places, including Abingdon, Canterbury and, most recently, Evesham; it has been connected with the house of Leofric, Earl of the North-West Midlands. D has information in particular about the west Midlands and northern England and is connected with Archbishop Ealdred of York. E, although it survives as part of a manuscript copied at Peterborough around 1120, is for the period 1043 to

1063 considered to have been a near-contemporary chronicle kept at St Augustine's, Canterbury; broadly speaking, it is more favourable to the Godwines, although it also expresses disagreement with some of their actions relating to the south-east.[1]

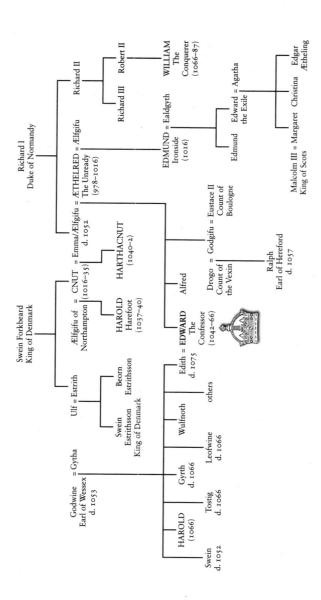

Map 1. England and North-west Europe
in the mid eleventh century

| 0 | 100 | 200 | 300 miles |
| 0 | 200 | 400 km |

ATLANTIC
OCEAN

Stiklestad

Shetland Is.

N
O
R
W
A
Y

Orkney Is.

S
W
E
D
E
N

SCOTLAND

Strathclyde

IRELAND

Northumbria

Dublin

Jelling

York

DENMARK

Wexford

Nottingham

Welsh
Kingships

ENGLAND

Mercia

Wolin

East
Anglia

Oxford

Wessex

London

Canterbury

Wulpe Bruges

Nijmegen

Wissant

Ghent

Meuse

Cologne

Saint-Riquier

Flanders

Fécamp

Rouen

Vexin

Bayeux

Jumièges

Elbe

Brittany

Normandy

Paris

Fulda

Angers

Le Mans

HOLY ROMAN
EMPIRE

Seine

Rhine

Tours

Loire

FRANCE

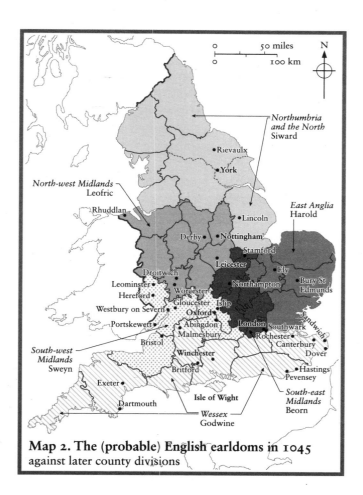

Map 2. The (probable) English earldoms in 1045
against later county divisions

Labels within the map:

50 miles
100 km
N

Northumbria and the North Siward

Rievaulx
York

North-west Midlands Leofric

Rhuddlan

Lincoln

East Anglia Harold

Derby • Nottingham
Stamford
Leicester • Ely
Northampton • Bury St Edmunds
Droitwich
Leominster • Worcester
Hereford • Gloucester • Islip
Westbury on Severn • Oxford
Portskewett • Abingdon • London Southwark
Bristol • Malmesbury • Rochester • Sandwich
Canterbury
South-west Midlands Sweyn
Winchester • Dover
Britford • Hastings
Pevensey
South-east Midlands Beorn
Exeter

Dartmouth **Isle of Wight**

Wessex Godwine

Edward the Confessor

I
Childhood and Exile

From the 990s, vikings were becoming an ever more serious threat to England's stability.* Æthelred the Unready, a king whose rule began in 978 and is traditionally judged in negative terms for his ultimate inability to defend the kingdom against Scandinavian attack, had had to deal with this external pressure almost from the very beginning of his reign. However, the 990s witnessed an escalation in terms not only of the severity of viking raids on England but also of their frequency. The *Anglo-Saxon Chronicle*, manuscript copies of which constitute vital sources for this period of history, records how in the year 1000 the vikings had sailed to Normandy, then ruled by Duke Richard II, in order to be better placed to continue their attacks on England the following summer.[1] This development evidently persuaded Æthelred of the desirability of some kind of alliance with Normandy. Two years later, in 1002 – his first wife, Ælfgifu of York, having either died or been put aside – he took Emma of Normandy, daughter of Richard I of Normandy and sister

---

* Since 'Viking', with an upper-case 'V', is suggestive of a distinct ethnic identity, 'viking(s)', with a lower-case 'v', is used throughout the book.

of Richard II, as his wife. Emma, who was then given the Old English name of Ælfgifu, thus became Queen of England and in due course mother to Edward the Confessor.

Edward was born at some point in the period 1003–5. We cannot be precise about the exact year or birthplace; Islip, Oxfordshire, is mentioned in a document from Westminster, though this has been thought to be a forgery.[2] He was the eldest son of Æthelred and Emma, with one younger sister, Godgifu, and one younger brother, Alfred. The anonymous author of the *Vita Ædwardi Regis* ('Life of King Edward') states that 'when the royal wife of old King Æthelred was pregnant in her womb, all the men of the country took an oath that if a man-child should come forth as the fruit of her labour, they would await in him their lord and king who would rule over the whole race of the English'.[3] But this text, written some sixty years after the birth of Edward, and in full knowledge of his subsequent attainment of the throne, conceals what must have been a much more complicated situation. For, given that Æthelred already had six sons by his previous marriage to Ælfgifu of York, there can have been little prospect that, when Edward was born, the new baby would ever become king. Æthelred was clearly a father who took great care in choosing names for his sons. Those born to his first wife were: Æthelstan (d. 1014), Ecgberht (d. 1005), Edmund (later known as 'Ironside', d. 1016), Eadred (d. 1012 × 1015), Eadwig (d. 1017) and Edgar (d. 1012 × 1015). 'Æthelstan' and 'Ecgberht' were names of particularly famous kings of the West Saxon line, while the other four replicate in the same sequence the names of kings of England from 939 (Edmund I) to 975 (Edgar).

What can be said of his choice of 'Edward' for his first son by Emma? One possibility is that he was named after King Edward the Elder (d. 924), famed for his warrior-like kingship and for his military exploits in capturing parts of the English Midlands settled by vikings. Another possibility is that he was named after Edward the Martyr, half-brother of Æthelred himself and King of England from 975 until he was murdered in March 978. A variety of evidence suggests that Æthelred, who succeeded him, and his advisers took particular interest in the Martyr, actively promoting his cult, in part as a means of bolstering the office of 'king' in the wake of this act of regicide.[4] Nevertheless, we should remember that Edward's younger brother was called 'Alfred', presumably in reference to that most famous of all Anglo-Saxon kings, Alfred the Great (d. 899), whose celebrity rested on his exploits in defending the kingdom from vikings. Perhaps Æthelred deliberately named his two sons by Emma after two kings of the West Saxon line who had previously won notable successes against viking armies.

We can imagine, then, that great hope had been placed in Edward from his birth, even if the prospect of his ever becoming king seemed remote. The formative years of Edward's youth were spent in a kingdom plagued by viking attack. The realities of this misery must have been horrifying: contemporaries talk of mass bloodshed, rape, famine and poverty, with the vikings seen as a punishment sent by God for the lax moral behaviour of the English. Raids in 1006–7 and 1009–12 seem to have been particularly severe, culminating in an event that was deeply shocking to the English: the capturing by the vikings of their Archbishop of

Canterbury, Ælfheah. In 1012 Ælfheah was murdered by a rabble of drunken vikings, and the *Anglo-Saxon Chronicle*, in its entry for this year, can hardly conceal its horror and disgust: 'they seized the bishop . . . and shamefully put him to death there: they pelted him with bones and with ox-heads, and one of them struck him on the head with the back of an axe, that he sank down with the blow, and his holy blood fell on the ground, and so he sent his holy soul to God's kingdom.'[5]

In the face of these atrocities, the king and his government tried a range of measures to avoid total defeat, offering increasingly large sums of money to the vikings so that they might leave, reorganizing administrative structures in the kingdom, and also – rather desperately – encouraging the English people to engage in acts of penitence in the hope that God might be appeased and the vikings might leave them in peace. As a young boy, Edward must have been deeply affected by these events. Royal diplomas (that is, official records of grants of land and/or privileges made by the king to beneficiaries) of the period 1005–13 record Edward's name among their lists of witnesses, suggesting that, whether or not the child was actually present at each particular meeting of the king's witan, he was nevertheless considered of sufficient importance that his name should be recorded among those attesting. Witness lists in Anglo-Saxon diplomas are laid out in rigidly hierarchical fashion, making it possible to chart the peaks and troughs of an individual's political career. It is instructive to find, therefore, that these diplomas contain the names of all of Æthelred's sons, from both of his marriages, and in strict order of age,

Æthelstan (the eldest) always being placed first. This must give us an indication of Edward's status relative to his half-brothers and brother throughout these years.

It is not beyond the realms of credibility that, towards the year 1013, a young Edward (then between seven and ten years old) was physically present at some meetings of the witan. If so, he would have heard discussion about royal policy and strategy for confronting the vikings, and witnessed his father giving voice to some of the major difficulties confronting him, in particular the machinations and betrayals of key individuals at his court. A twelfth-century text from Ely preserves the tradition that Edward, as a baby, had been given by his mother and father to Ely Abbey, where he was brought up with other boys and taught the 'psalms and hymns of the Lord'.[6] There is reason to be cautious about this tale, not least because one of its functions is to create the idea of a special relationship between Edward and Ely so that the narration of a subsequent gift of lands by Edward to the abbey makes better sense. But scholars have not dismissed it outright and a link between Ely and the royal court is provided in the form of Saint Æthelwold (d. 984). Instrumental in the monastic reform movement of the mid tenth century, Æthelwold was also Æthelred's tutor at one time and closely connected with Ely itself. Edward may have spent part of his childhood in the fenlands of East Anglia.[7] While this cannot be verified, he is afterwards found under the care of a certain Leofrun, his 'foster-mother' (foster-moder), if a writ in the name of Edward from later in his reign may be believed.[8]

The events of 1013 had a profound impact on the young

Edward's life. A vivid entry in the *Anglo-Saxon Chronicle* records the invasion, just before August, of King Swein Forkbeard of Denmark. Arriving with a fleet first at the port of Sandwich, Swein sailed round the coast of East Anglia and into the River Humber, before turning south again and sailing up the River Trent as far as Gainsborough. Swein's very presence caused the Northumbrians and their earl (a man named Uhtred) to surrender to him. This was followed shortly afterwards by the capitulation of the territory known as the Five Boroughs (comprising Derby, Leicester, Lincoln, Nottingham and Stamford) and of 'all the Danish settlers north of Watling Street' (a Roman road running from north-west to south-east that served also as a territorial boundary). At this point Swein turned his attention southwards, his army ravaging as it went, to such an extent that the citizens of Oxford and Winchester also surrendered to him. London, which was where Æthelred then had his court, at first offered the most resistance to Swein's progress, but, following the submission of the south-west, the Londoners also admitted defeat. England bowed to the inevitable and Swein was declared king.[9]

Swein's conquest had major consequences for Æthelred's family that would affect Edward for the next twenty-five years of his life. First of all, Edward's mother, Emma, fled across the Channel to the Norman court of her brother, Duke Richard II, accompanied by Abbot Ælfsige of Peterborough. Meanwhile, Æthelred ordered the Bishop of London, Ælfhun, to take Edward and his brother Alfred in a separate party 'across the sea . . . that he should take care of them'.[10] We do not know why Edward and Alfred were separated from their mother at this stage: perhaps it was thought prudent to separate the parties in case something happened to the queen or the æthelings (royal princes) during what could be a perilous sea voyage. Æthelred himself also left London, spending Christmas on the Isle of Wight, before himself proceeding to the court of Richard in Normandy.

As events transpired, Swein died on 3 February 1014, not long after the flight of Æthelred from England. Swein's army elected his son, Cnut, as king. But members of the witan had a different view and approached King Æthelred in the hope that he would return from Normandy to reclaim his rule in England. It is at this moment that the *Anglo-Saxon Chronicle* gives us the first indication that Edward, though still a young boy, now played some role in high politics. For Æthelred, in response to the request of the witan, sent his son and a group of messengers to negotiate the terms of the king's return.[11] Edward, then a boy of between eight and eleven years of age, is unlikely to have had an active role in the discussions that followed; it is more likely that his presence was designed to guarantee that Æthelred sincerely meant whatever promises he had offered. The negotiations were a success. Both parties swore oaths to each other and Æthelred, together with Emma and their sons Edward and Alfred, returned to England in the spring.

The *Anglo-Saxon Chronicle* recounts how the rest of 1014 witnessed Æthelred's attempts to remove Cnut from the kingdom, culminating in Cnut's setting sail with his forces but then landing at Sandwich to drop off the hostages that had been in his father's possession and how there he 'cut off their hands, ears, and noses'.[12] Such barbarity was a fore-taste of what was to come, as the next two years were marked by repeated conflicts between Cnut and the English. Many atrocities were committed as power shifted at one moment to Æthelred and his followers, and at other times to Cnut and his men. Edward can hardly have played a significant part in the events of 1014–16, but his half-brother Edmund took up his father's cause with vigour. Following Æthelred's death on 23 April 1016, he was elected king and 'stoutly defended his kingdom while his life lasted',[13] thus earning himself the honorific 'Ironside'. Edmund fought five battles against the vikings. But the last battle, which took place on 18 October at a hill of an uncertain location known as 'Assandun', saw Edmund crucially weakened by the treacherous flight of the powerful and notorious Eadric Streona. Cnut proved victorious and the *Anglo-Saxon Chronicle* makes the hyperbolic statement that 'all the nobility of England was there destroyed'.[14]

Although rulership of the kingdom was for a time divided between Edmund and Cnut, Edmund's death on 30 November 1016 meant that Cnut became king of all England. Crowned in 1017, Cnut immediately took measures to secure his position: he divided England into four earldoms (Wessex, East Anglia, Mercia and Northumbria); he had Eadric Streona executed for his treachery, along with other key individuals; and he took special care to make sure that surviving members of the royal dynasty were removed from the scene. Eadwig, the only surviving son of Æthelred by his first wife, was sent into exile, and, on his return to England later, was killed on Cnut's order. Cnut also targeted the sons of Edmund Ironside – Edward and Edmund – and, fearful of incurring the shame of killing them himself, sent them instead to the King of Sweden to be murdered. In the event, the Swedish king likewise could not bring himself to carry out Cnut's orders and so passed Edward and Edmund on to the King of Hungary, a man called Stephen.[15] We will meet this Edward again later.

What was the fate of Æthelred's own sons, Edward and his younger brother Alfred? It seems likely that they also fled the kingdom soon after the death of Edmund in late 1016. And in fact a rather remarkable manuscript – a copy made in the 1040s and preserved in the archives of St Peter's Abbey in Ghent of a document dated 25 December 1016 – provides unusual detail about Edward's movements and intentions at this time. If it can be accepted as genuine, the copy provides extraordinary testimony of what the monks at St Peter's Abbey in the 1040s thought had happened in 1016. The copy, which records an oath made in the name of Edward when he visited the abbey in Ghent at Christmas that year, suggests, at the very least, that he had found it necessary to leave England immediately after Edmund's death and had sought refuge in Flanders. As part of the oath, Edward declares that he was visiting saintly places in the hope that the Lord might pardon him and return him to his father's kingdom. When he arrived at St Peter's Abbey, according to the copy, the abbot (a man named Rodbold) and the monks welcomed him and told him about certain estates that had belonged to them in England but that had been unjustly taken from them. In response, Edward makes a promise at the altar in the abbey that he will reinstate these estates to the community if he himself can return to his father's kingdom.[16]

Standing at the altar of St Peter's Abbey in Ghent on 25 December 1016, Edward could not have known that he would spend the next twenty-five years or so in exile on the continent. His mother, Emma, who had probably been left behind in London, managed to guarantee her own position in this new political order by marrying Cnut himself.[17] It is plausible that Cnut saw his marriage to Emma as an opportunity to demonstrate continuity with the previous regime, but no doubt there were other reasons too. One highly partisan text, known as the *Encomium Emmae Reginae* ('Praise of Queen Emma'), states that a condition of this marriage for Emma was that Cnut would only set up as king a son of their own union and that sons by other marriages had no claim.[18] If true, this meant that, as things stood, Edward had been removed from the line of succession. In the first two years of his reign, then, Cnut took a series of measures designed to strengthen his position, many of which were to Edward's detriment. This was a new world, and opportunities were there for new men, not least one by the name of Godwine, who by 1018 had been given an earldom (probably in eastern Wessex) and by 1023 had become the most senior lay figure at Cnut's witan. Godwine and his family, as we shall see, were to become hugely powerful by the end of the Anglo-Saxon period. The roots of their power were laid in this period of Scandinavian rule.

Edward, even if he was not aware of the exact details of these changes in England, must nevertheless have been all too conscious of the politically isolated position that he and his brother now occupied. As it turned out, the two of them were to spend all of Cnut's reign in Normandy. Their uncle Duke Richard II (r. 966–1026) and their cousins Richard III (r. 1026–7) and Robert I (r. 1027–35) provided them with support. While it is difficult to reconstruct this period of exile in any kind of detail, it is clear that the Normans held the æthelings in high regard, thinking of them as princes of royal blood who had been denied their rightful inheritance. The *Inuentio et Miracula Sancti Vulfranni* ('The Discovery and Miracles of Saint Vulfran'), written at the abbey of Saint-Wandrille in the early to mid 1050s, constitutes a Norman account of relations between Normandy and England in the early eleventh century.[19] Notable for its claim that Edward, while still a young boy in England, had been consecrated king, it also states that he was Richard II's nephew (and was thus related to him by blood), that the æthelings were treated generously at his court, as if they were the duke's own sons, and that as long as they lived in Normandy they were received with great honour. Two other Norman authors – William of Jumièges and William of Poitiers – also describe the support offered by successive dukes of Normandy to Edward and Alfred.[20] And William of Jumièges likewise describes Edward as a 'king' (*rex*) during this period of exile.[21]

Tantalizing evidence survives from the early 1030s that gives us a clear indication of Edward's own views about his claim at this stage to the English throne. Appended to a charter in the name of Duke Robert I of Normandy in which he grants properties and rights to the abbey of Fécamp is a list of witnesses beginning with the name of the duke himself and followed by that of his son, William (added after the original drafting of the witness list, directly below Robert's name), and those of various other dignitaries, both secular and ecclesiastical. At the right-hand side of the document, added after the initial writing of the witness list, is the phrase 'The sign of Edward the king' (*Signum Eduuardi regis*), next to which seems to be a cross made by Edward himself. We could not wish for clearer proof that Edward – willing to put his own mark next to the title 'king' (*regis*) – believed in his claim to the throne of England while he was in exile in Normandy. Even more striking is how his name appears here alongside that of William, the very man who would later conquer England in 1066.[22]

It was clearly of benefit to Edward (and Alfred) to garner strong support from Norman allies. And the marriage of their sister, Godgifu, in April 1024 to Drogo, Count of the Vexin (a strategically important area of north-western France between Rouen and Paris), shows how deeply enmeshed in Norman politics the siblings were becoming. William of Jumièges tells us that Duke Robert was so strong an advocate of the æthelings that 'he sent envoys to King Cnut with the request that since their exile had been sufficiently long he should be merciful and return to them, however late, what was theirs for the love of him [i.e. Robert]'. When Cnut refused the duke's requests, Robert, 'enraged by fury, called together the magnates of his duchy and gave orders that a great fleet should instantly be formed'; the evidence of charters suggests that this fleet may have been gathered in about Easter 1033.[23] If this attempted invasion came to anything, it has left no record in English sources. But clearly the Norman dukes, whatever their exact motivations, were willing to offer both military and financial aid to Edward in staking his claim to the English throne.[24] The Norman sources' emphasis on Edward's kinship to the Norman dukes would later form an important part of their justification for Norman claims to the throne of England itself, as we will see in Chapter 4.

The death of Cnut in 1035 set in motion a succession crisis. It had reportedly been a condition of his marriage to Emma that only a son of their union – Harthacnut, that is – could succeed as the next king. But, at the crucial moment of Cnut's death, Harthacnut, then about eighteen years old, had been delayed in Denmark. At a meeting at Oxford there were those leading men who therefore advocated that Harold Harefoot (son of Cnut by Ælfgifu of Northampton) should be crowned, and those, including Godwine and Emma herself, who opposed this suggestion.[25] In the end, an agreement seems to have been reached whereby Harold Harefoot, supported by Earl Leofric, would rule in the north of the kingdom and Queen Emma and Earl Godwine would rule in the south, on behalf of Harthacnut in his absence.

Despite the agreement at Oxford for rule to be shared between Harold Harefoot and Harthacnut, the political situation was much disturbed and Emma may have felt increasingly isolated. One chronicler for the year 1035 records how Harold ensured that she was deprived of her possessions at Winchester.[26] The following year saw the dramatic re-emergence of the æthelings (Edward and his brother Alfred) on to the English political scene. There is some uncertainty as to whether it was their own choice to return to England, seeking to take advantage of the

succession crisis, or whether they were invited back by
Emma herself, who may have been discomfited by Harthacnut's continued absence and was therefore looking for new
political allies. The existence of a letter in Emma's name,
inserted in her *Encomium* – and discussed below – makes
it the more likely that the æthelings came back at their
mother's request. According to contemporary accounts,
Edward and Alfred arrived separately. Edward sailed with
forty ships to Southampton, and, having achieved a military
victory there, returned quite quickly to Normandy in the
face of a large English force; Alfred, however, first went from
Normandy to Wissant in Flanders and then crossed to
Dover,[27] penetrating further into the English kingdom than
his brother. But what happened next was to colour English
politics for the generation to follow. It seems that Alfred and
his men, while trying to reach Emma at Winchester, were
met and at first peacefully received by Earl Godwine. But
Godwine then betrayed Alfred by delivering him into the
hands of Harold Harefoot. The *Anglo-Saxon Chronicle*
records that Alfred was placed in bonds and taken to Ely,
where, 'as soon as he arrived, he was blinded on the ship, and
thus blind was brought to the monks'.[28] Alfred's mutilation
resulted in his death the following year on 5 February 1037.

By early 1037, then, the situation must have seemed bleak
for Edward. His brother, betrayed by Godwine, had been
tortured and later died from his wounds, and his own
expedition the previous year had revealed the scale of attack
that would be required to secure his return to England. Harold Harefoot was then chosen as king for the whole kingdom
and Edward's mother, Emma, was herself driven into exile,

crossing the sea to Bruges, where she found refuge at the court of Baldwin V, Count of Flanders (d. 1067).[29] It must have seemed to Edward that his claim to the English throne was further than ever from his grasp. The *Encomium Emmae Reginae* suggests that Emma, once in Bruges, was visited by Edward but that, since he was unable to help her, she turned once more to her other son, Harthacnut.[30] Edward is said to have returned to Normandy, while Harthacnut journeyed in 1039 to Bruges to join his mother.

The status quo did not last long. The death of Harold Harefoot in 1040 prompted the English to send 'to Bruges for Harthacnut, thinking that they were acting wisely'.[31] Harthacnut duly returned to England with Emma, who resumed her position at the centre of affairs in England. But Harthacnut's time as king was not well received, the *Anglo-Saxon Chronicle* recording that 'all who had wanted him before were then ill-disposed towards him. And also he did nothing worthy of a king as long as he ruled.'[32] There is evidence to suggest that in the years 1040–41 there was resentment also about what had been done in Harold Harefoot's reign. Harthacnut himself, 'remembering the injuries which his predecessor King Harold, who was considered his brother, had perpetrated against both him and his mother',[33] ordered that Harold's body be exhumed and 'thrown into a fen'.[34] At the same time Ælfric, the Archbishop of York, accused Earl Godwine and Lyfing, Bishop of Worcester, of being responsible for the death of the ætheling Alfred. In the face of this accusation, Godwine in particular is described as going to great lengths to try to secure royal favour, swearing on oath that he had not wanted Alfred to be blinded, but that he was only acting on the orders of King Harold.[35] It is clear that the death of Edward's brother, Alfred, had left a bitter legacy. There were many in England in the opening years of the 1040s who deeply resented what had happened and who were suspicious of anyone connected with it, most particularly Godwine himself. It may also be that criticism was directed at Alfred's mother for her possible role in calling back the æthelings from Normandy in 1036, since the *Encomium Emmae Reginae*, composed at Emma's behest, goes to extraordinary lengths to exculpate her and distance her from any involvement, including the insertion of a letter said to have been forged in her name and written at the command of Harold to lure the æthelings to England.[36]

In the midst of this political chaos, the *Anglo-Saxon Chronicle* records for the year 1041 that 'there came from beyond the sea Edward, his [i.e. Harthacnut's] brother on the mother's side, the son of King Æthelred, who had been driven from his country many years before – and yet he was sworn in as king; and thus he stayed at his brother's court as long as he lived'.[37] We can imagine that the invitation to Edward to return was engineered by Harthacnut and Emma in order both to restore peace to England and once more to make it clear that Emma had not been involved in the events of 1036. It may also have been designed to placate any lingering grievances over the maltreatment of Alfred. Writing from the perspective of 1041–2, the author of the *Encomium Emmae Reginae* describes this period of joint rule between Emma, Harthacnut and Edward in superficially positive terms: 'Here there is loyalty among sharers of rule, here the bond of motherly and brotherly love is of strength indestructible.'[38] But, with the expression 'here there is loyalty among sharers of rule', the author is alluding to a well-known line from Lucan's *De Bello Civili* ('On the Civil War'), in which the Roman epicist *denies* the likelihood of loyalty in a partnership of power: thus is indicated the author's own foreboding about the realities of the co-rule adopted by Harthacnut and Edward.[39]

A rather surprising source – the preface to a collection of Old English laws translated into Latin in the early twelfth century – provides more detail about the kind of support that Edward himself had managed to gather in England in 1041:

> At length, Edward, son of King Æthelred, was recalled, through the intervention of Bishop Ælfwine of Winchester and Earl Godwine; the thegns of all England gathered together at *Hursteshevet*, and there it was heard that he would be received as king only if he guarantee to them upon oath that the laws of Cnut and his sons should continue in his time with unshaken firmness.[40]

Although written after the Anglo-Saxon period, the evidence provided by the preface is regarded as reliable by modern historians. The primary interest for us lies in its assertion that Edward was being considered as Harthacnut's successor not just by those at the highest levels of English government, but also by the 'thegns of all England', the term 'thegn' designating men of a noble rank in society.

On 8 June 1042, Harthacnut died while drinking at a wedding feast at Lambeth.[41] In a brief entry, the

Anglo-Saxon Chronicle records: 'and all the people then received Edward as king, as was his natural right'.[42] Edward had finally attained the position he had been seeking ever since his departure from England many years before. But, as we will see, his long period of exile meant that he lacked the usual advantages of a natural power base and could not automatically rely on those around him. His own mother proved herself politically unreliable and she rushed once again to guarantee her position in the wake of Harthacnut's death, giving her encomiast the task of rewriting the original ending to his work. Only recently discovered by scholars, this new conclusion seeks to redirect the spotlight from Harthacnut and Edward as joint rulers to Edward as the true heir to the throne:

> Indeed with Harthacnut dead Edward succeeded to the kingdom, namely the legitimate heir, a man notable for the eminence of his power, endowed with virtue of mind and counsel and also with quickness of intellect, and – to conclude in brief – marked out by the sum of all desirable things. At his coming, the whole land was hushed and bent its neck ready to be pressed down under his dominion's heel. For it had previously longed a thousand times with a thousand prayers for the day of his lordship, since it saw shining out in him the mark of his father's goodness and wisdom.[43]

Although this passage gives the impression of a kingdom united in its longing for Edward's rule, the reality was very different. Edward had much to do and his position in mid June 1042 must have felt less than secure.

2

Accession and Power

Following the death of Harthacnut in June 1042, Edward was received as king by the English. But it was not until 3 April 1043, nearly a year later, that he was consecrated king, at Winchester on Easter Day.[1] Although we cannot be certain, it is possible that the length of the delay was caused by the difficulties and insecurities of Edward's position upon becoming king.[2] The previous two reigns (of Harold Harefoot and Harthacnut) had shown all too clearly how destabilized domestic politics had become, and the support of different members of the ruling elite, both secular and ecclesiastical, could not be guaranteed. Edward's long period of exile meant, as we have seen, that he lacked a natural base of support in England and, although he would have brought companions and advisers with him from Normandy, it is unlikely that there were enough of them initially to tip the balance in his favour among factions at the royal court.[3] Insufficient support at home would have been compounded by the continued threat of invasion from abroad, with Magnus, King of Norway, harbouring claims to the English throne, bands of vikings still exerting pressure on the English coastline and Count Baldwin V of Flanders offering refuge to many of England's political exiles and enemies.

Edward had to proceed with the utmost care and there are indications that he and his advisers took measures to project an image of strong kingship. Even if Edward's consecration had had to be delayed, there was much to be gained by holding it on Easter Day itself.[4] Following a sequence of Scandinavian incumbents on the English throne, Edward represented the resurrection of the line of English kings that had prospered before the likes of Swein Forkbeard and Cnut. Winchester, which had constituted the symbolic heart of the kingdom in the tenth century, must have been chosen in order to complement this message. Eadsige, the Archbishop of Canterbury, and perhaps also Ælfric, the Archbishop of York, presided over the ceremony, at which Edward would have been required to make a pledge at the altar in the church. Following a liturgical rite first used for the coronation of kings in the tenth century, Edward made a three-fold promise to his subjects: that under his rule the Church and all Christian people in his dominion would keep the peace; that robbery and all unrighteous deeds would be forbidden; and that justice and mercy in all judgements would be observed. A near-contemporary sermon about royal coronation promises indicates that any king who upheld his coronation pledge would be assured worldly glory and divine favour in the eternal life.[5] The consecration had been carefully choreographed to project the image of Edward as a king able to bring renewed political stability to England.

Such an image would have been reinforced by Edward's coinage, which offered a very potent means of communicating political messages to his new subjects. The first coins from his reign to survive are a few specimens of the type known as 'Arm and Sceptre' pennies. These are the same kind as those issued in the years 1040–42 during the reign of his predecessor, Harthacnut. Either those in charge of producing the coins simply continued with the same design in order to minimize the changes needed, or it was a deliberate decision by the king to continue with the coinage that was then current. Whatever the case, the 'Arm and Sceptre' pennies had a limited lifespan (perhaps in circulation only during the summer of 1042) and seem quickly to have been replaced in 1042 by the 'Pacx' type, which lasted until the mid 1040s.[6] On the obverse side of the coin the king is depicted in a left-facing bust and with a sceptre, while on the reverse side the letters P, A, C, X each appear in separate quarters of the coin divided by a central cross, to spell *Pacx* ('Peace'). These coins, taking inspiration in their iconography ultimately from Roman coins and from near-contemporary royal diplomas, were designed to promote the idea of peace through reference to Christ.

Despite this projection of stability, the reality of Edward's position may have been rather different. A measure of the insecurity he must have felt is perhaps provided by one of his first recorded acts as king: an attack in 1043 on his duplicitous mother, Emma, who, as under Harold in 1035, was deprived of her possessions – this time all her lands and movable wealth. Emma's close supporter Stigand, a royal priest who had only recently been made Bishop of Elmham, was also targeted, being removed from office and stripped of his possessions; it was felt that he had influenced Emma too much.[7] These developments were not in themselves surprising. Emma had been centrally involved in the politics of the preceding years and had been less than supportive of Edward, turning to him when in need, but abandoning him when it suited her. This is to say nothing of her possible role in the return of her son Alfred in 1036, whose torture and subsequent death were a stain on her character which, as we have seen, her *Encomium* went to great lengths to try to remove. At Canterbury later in the eleventh century, it was recorded that Emma may even have been involved in encouraging Magnus, King of Norway, to invade England, claiming that she had given him great riches. It would be hazardous to accept this account at face value, but its articulation demonstrates the suspicion that lingered over Emma's behaviour.[8] What *is* surprising is that Edward needed the support of the three leading earls – Leofric (of the north-west Midlands), Godwine (of Wessex) and Siward (of Northumbria) – in order to carry out his plan.[9] Emma herself seems to have been permitted to remain living in Winchester and, at least until 1045, she continues to attest royal documents with the Latin title *mater regis* or its Old English equivalent *hlæfdige*, both meaning 'queen mother' (*hlæfdige* – an Old English compound noun composed of the words *hlæf* or 'loaf' and *dige* or 'kneader' – being the origin of our modern word 'lady').

It was extremely important that Edward garnered the support of his earls, who were very significant figures in eleventh-century England. As royal officials, they were in charge of their earldoms, which had changing geographical boundaries, and provided a conduit for royal business, decided at meetings of the king's witan, from the centre of the kingdom to its localities, where they took charge, on behalf of the king, of matters such as the enforcement of law and order. There was no set number of earls, and different kings had different approaches to the kinds of men appointed. Because the earls were able to draw on their own lands, resources and military forces, and because they were invested with such a large amount of authority that they were the highest-ranking secular officials in the kingdom, they had the potential to cause the king (and their rival earls) huge difficulties. As we will see, Edward's relations with his earls were to remain a primary concern throughout his reign.

In the early to mid 1040s, the three leading earls in England – Godwine, Leofric and Siward – had not been appointed by Edward. He had inherited them from the reigns of his predecessors. Having to accept Godwine must have been a bitter pill for Edward to swallow. It would have been impossible to forget the earl's purported involvement in the death of his own brother; he must also have been aware that Godwine's real sympathies were more likely to rest with a Scandinavian pretender to the throne rather than Edward himself. Godwine's career had been formed in the court of King Cnut and he had been a prominent supporter of Harthacnut in 1035. His wife, Gytha, had a background in the Danish ruling elite: her nephew was Swein Estrithsson, who became King of Denmark in 1047 and who had ongoing connections with England throughout this period.[10] Their four eldest sons, who were to have such a major impact on the kingdom's politics, had been given predominantly Scandinavian names – Swein, Harold, Tostig and Gyrth – while their two youngest sons, Leofwine and Wulfnoth, bore Old English names.

While Edward could not have been anything other than suspicious of Godwine's intentions, he nevertheless needed the earl's support upon his accession. As Earl of Wessex, the heart of the English kingdom, Godwine was hugely influential. And, from as early as 1023 through to the beginning of Edward's reign in 1042 and beyond, Godwine consistently attested royal documents as the highest-ranking secular official. His power had been deeply entrenched within and across the reigns of different kings, and the benefits of having him as a supporter would have been plain. Godwine, too, would have been keen to win the king's favour, as revealed by the *Vita Ædwardi*, itself commissioned by Edith, Godwine's daughter, and later Edward's wife, and written towards the end of Edward's reign or just afterwards. Combining passages of both prose and verse, the *Vita* includes a poem, the full text of which has only recently come to light, describing the gift of a great ship to Edward from Godwine following the king's coronation. With 'the long curves of its sides drawn together to two high points', the ship

stood on the winding Thames, its many benches in evenly spaced order. The lofty mast placed amidships looked down on the fittings for a hundred and twice ten menacing heroes. A golden lion stands up at the stern, while in the prow a golden dragon, its body winged, frightens the seas, spewing out flames from threefold mouth. The hung sail, noble in

precious purple, has painted on it the succession of fore-
bears to give instruction, alongside the wars of noble kings
on the troubled seas.[11]

Gifts of such a lavish nature were not made without good
reason. If we take this poem literally (rather than figura-
tively), that Godwine had provided Edward with such a
ship, it is indicative of the extent of his desire to win over
the king; it was surely also demonstrative of the great guilt
that the earl felt for his involvement in the death of
Edward's brother.[12]

In the early years of his reign, Edward made sure that
Earl Godwine was on his side. In 1043, Swein, Godwine's
eldest son, was made Earl of the South-West Midlands
and, by 1045, Godwine's second son, Harold, was made
Earl of East Anglia and his nephew, Beorn Estrithsson,
Earl of the South-East Midlands. These appointments con-
solidated the power of the house of Godwine in the south
of England, while Leofric and Siward continued to hold
the north-west Midlands and Northumbria respectively.
The appointment of Beorn, brother of Swein Estrithsson
(King of Denmark from 1047), may well have been driven
by the demands of diplomacy, in order to minimize the risk
of attack from Denmark.

The year 1045 saw a further advance in the house of
Godwine's power, for Edward took as his wife Edith, the
daughter of Earl Godwine.[13] The *Vita Ædwardi* naturally
goes to great lengths to stress what a good choice she was.
In a prose passage that is missing from the surviving copy
of the text, but has been reconstructed by a modern editor

from the work of two writers of the medieval period who themselves drew on the *Vita*, Edith is described in exceedingly complimentary terms as 'famous and distinguished for verse and prose, and in her needlework and painting . . . another Minerva'.[14] The comparison with Minerva, Roman goddess of, among other things, craft and wisdom, was intended to demonstrate the suitability of Edith as a match for Edward. But the *Vita* itself betrays the real reasons for the union: 'Edward agreed all the more readily to contract this marriage because he knew that with the advice and help of that Godwine he would have a firmer hold on his hereditary rights in England.'[15] This was above all a marriage of political expediency. Having succeeded to the throne following a long period of exile, Edward needed the support of the leading noble family and, by 1045, he had successfully secured it. As we will see, however, the relationship between the king and the Godwines was not to continue harmoniously. To the contrary, it broke down in most dramatic fashion. And the fact that the marriage between Edward and Edith ultimately remained childless (a feature later exploited in tales in which Edward's sanctity is attributed partly to his chastity) caused great uncertainty for the future of the English throne, with many interested parties thereby enabled to advance their claim.

After describing Edward and Edith's marriage, and the crowning of Edith as queen, the *Vita Ædwardi* continues by saying that, on his return from exile in Normandy, Edward had brought a number of men with him whom he 'enriched . . . with many honours, and made them his privy counsellors and administrators of the royal palace'.[16] It is natural that

Edward would have brought some supporters with him from the continent, even if not in large numbers and even if the majority of the king's early household contained men who had served also under Cnut and Harthacnut.[17] It is possible that some members of the royal court conducted business in French. Among the names of continental supporters recorded from the beginning of Edward's reign are, most prominently, Robert, Abbot of Jumièges, and Edward's own nephew Ralph of Mantes, the son of Godgifu and her first husband, Drogo, Count of the Vexin. Robert was a close ally and confidant of the king and played a major role in various episodes during the reign; he was closely associated with what – to some contemporaries – became the 'foreign' faction at Edward's court and would later be resented by those who represented the 'old guard' (that is, the Godwines and their supporters). Later in the reign, Ralph became Earl of the South-East Midlands. Edward also had enemies upon his accession, perhaps particularly those who identified most strongly with the previous regimes of Scandinavian monarchs. The *Anglo-Saxon Chronicle* reveals the actions that Edward took to confront his rivals: in 1044 the lady Gunnild, related to King Cnut, was banished and subsequently sought refuge in Bruges before heading to Denmark; and, in 1046, a nobleman by the name of Osgod Clapa, who had formed his career under Cnut, was likewise exiled from the kingdom.[18] Osgod clearly constituted a very real threat, for we learn that in 1049 he gathered a fleet of ships at Wulpe in Flanders in order to attack England.[19]

In church politics, Edward seems to have attempted, where possible, to influence appointments to office as and when different bishoprics became vacant. In 1044 Eadsige, Archbishop of Canterbury, became unwell and an unusual solution to this crisis seems to have been found. We are told that Siward, then Abbot of Abingdon, was 'consecrated to it [i.e. Canterbury] as bishop',[20] and he subsequently acted in agreement with Eadsige, sometimes being accorded archiepiscopal status in Eadsige's absence, but always relegated to a lower status whenever Eadsige was able to be present. What is striking about this solution is that it was effected jointly by Earl Godwine and Edward and kept secret from the majority of people, so that no rival claimant could be put forward.[21] The *Anglo-Saxon Chronicle* records in the same year the death of Ælfweard, Bishop of London, who had held this episcopal see while simultaneously holding the abbacy of Evesham. The combined testimony of the *Anglo-Saxon Chronicle* and John of Worcester's *Chronicle* provides the detail that a monk from Evesham, Wulfmær (known also as Mannig), was elected abbot in his place. But it is striking that no details are given about Ælfweard's replacement as Bishop of London.[22] It is only when we turn to royal documents of the period (diplomas) and to the *Vita Ædwardi* that we find that Ælfweard had been replaced by Robert of Jumièges, Edward's trusted confidant at this stage. Given that Ælfweard is thought to have been related to King Cnut, and that he was a strong supporter of Harthacnut, it may be that Edward was taking the opportunity of his death to hand the strategically important London bishopric to an individual who was more likely to see things from the royal point of view.

Until the end of the 1040s, Edward himself is recorded as

being in charge of selecting new bishops for episcopal sees and he tended to appoint men from the royal household. Thus Hereman, from Lotharingia, the king's chaplain, received the Ramsbury bishopric in 1045; Leofric, an Englishman educated in Lotharingia, also described as the king's chaplain, was made Bishop of Devon and Cornwall in 1046; Heca, another priest from the royal household, received the Sussex bishopric in 1047; and Ulf, a Norman, and also the king's chaplain, was given the Dorchester bishopric in 1049. Edward was therefore taking the opportunities as they arose of staffing the major churches in England with men naturally loyal to himself who would be influential both at meetings of the witan and in their local regions. By 1050 the majority of bishops owed their positions directly to the king's influence. It is less clear, however, that Edward was able to make such changes when it came to the highest level of secular governance. We have already seen the lengths to which he went in order to curry favour with Earl Godwine and his family; and it is mainly members of that family who received earldoms in the period 1042–50. The two other major earls whom Edward inherited from his predecessors' reigns, Leofric in the north-west Midlands and Siward in Northumbria, kept their power throughout these years. It was not until 1050 that a new appointment was made from outside the Godwine family, when Ralph of Mantes, Edward's nephew, began operating as earl.

During the years 1043–9 Edward had to think not only of England, but also of events that were unfolding in north-west Europe. The *Vita Ædwardi* suggests that, on his accession, various continental rulers, including Henry III (who became emperor in 1046), Henry I, King of the French, and Swein Estrithsson, King of Denmark, sent ambassadors to England in order to confirm bonds of alliance between them and the new English king.[23] Edward also had the support of his brother-in-law, Eustace II, who would become Count of Boulogne in 1049, and who was later involved in the critical events of 1051.[24] But there were those who were not so sympathetic to Edward's rule. We have already encountered the rumours of a potential invasion of England by Magnus of Norway, and at times England was also involved in the struggle between Magnus and Swein Estrithsson over the control of Denmark. Likewise Baldwin V, Count of Flanders, repeatedly offered refuge to England's political enemies throughout these years. In the circumstances, Edward was keen to assert himself. We are told of numerous occasions on which he himself took command of a fleet of ships and made displays of military might. For example, in 1045, at the important port of Sandwich, Edward's fleet was so great that 'no one had ever seen a larger naval force in this country'.[25] Such a force was required because of the threat posed by Magnus, even if in the end the fighting between Magnus and Swein in Denmark meant that the risk to England subsided.[26] Events came to a head in 1047. Under pressure, Swein asked Edward to help him by sending fifty ships. If the testimony of a later source can be accepted, it suggests that opinion may have been divided on whether or not to help Swein. John of Worcester's *Chronicle* states that Godwine, Swein's uncle, advised Edward to provide the support that Swein needed, whereas this was opposed by 'Earl Leofric and all the people', with the result that no ships were sent from England.[27] It is not hard to discern the reasons for Godwine's stance; he was presumably partly motivated to help someone related to him and partly in the interests of his own position. We can assume that Edward ultimately made the decision that was in his, and the kingdom's, best interests. Edward's ignoring of Godwine's advice may also have formed an early indication that the Godwine party was becoming less favoured. Magnus had control in Denmark, but his death later in 1047 meant that he could no longer threaten England.

The menace to England's coastline remained, however. In 1048 a viking fleet led by two men, Lothen and Yrling, arrived at Sandwich and 'captured an indescribable amount of plunder in men and gold and silver, so that nobody knew how much it was altogether'.[28] The raiders continued round the eastern coast and ravaged parts of Essex, before setting off to the court of Count Baldwin V of Flanders to sell the loot that they had seized. In 1049 Emperor Henry III, incensed both by an attack on the palace of Nijmegen and by numerous other aggressive acts, gathered a large army against Baldwin. In doing so, the emperor requested naval reinforcements from Edward to prevent Baldwin from fleeing across the sea. This time Edward, sensing an opportunity to neutralize future threats from Flanders, agreed, and again positioned himself at Sandwich with a large fleet, remaining there for as long as he was needed.[29]

Meanwhile, there was trouble in England too. The year 1046 witnessed the first of a succession of aggressive acts by

Swein, Godwine's eldest son, which led to tensions between the Godwines themselves and perhaps encouraged Edward to reconsider the amount of power that he had vested in this family. In 1046 Swein joined the Welsh king, Gruffudd ap Llywelyn, on a joint military expedition in Wales; on his return, he abducted the Abbess of Leominster and kept her with him for 'as long as it suited him, and then he let her go home'.[30] It is likely that Swein's actions were designed to threaten Earl Leofric and to diminish his influence on the Welsh Marches. Swein's Welsh ally, King Gruffudd, had been directly responsible for the death of Leofric's brother Edwin in 1039 and Leofric had taken a particular interest in cultivating relations with the Leominster nunnery. The fact that in 1047 Swein, seemingly as a result of his actions, was forced to flee to Count Baldwin in Bruges and then on to Denmark suggests that there were those in England, perhaps Edward himself, who strongly disapproved of what he had done.[31]

In 1049 Swein returned to England. At first he tried to ask Edward for his favour and to be restored to his previous positions of power. At this point it seems that Swein's own brother Harold and his cousin Beorn may have opposed the earl's requests because they stood to lose those lands that had previously been forfeited by Swein upon his flight to the continent and which had been transferred to them, with the result that the king also denied Swein's wishes. Swein then approached Godwine and Beorn, who were with their ships at Pevensey, in Sussex, petitioning Beorn to accompany him to meet the king at Sandwich, on the pretext that Beorn would be able to help him make peace with Edward. Swein and Beorn journeyed to Bosham, where Swein's ships were anchored, but, instead of proceeding to Sandwich, Beorn was seized by Swein's men and taken to Dartmouth, where he was promptly killed. One version of the *Anglo-Saxon Chronicle* then records that the 'king and all the host declared Swein an outcast' and that he fled once more to the protection of Baldwin in Flanders.[32]

Swein's actions in 1046–9 reveal that he at least was not prepared to toe the establishment line. He seems not to have been acting with the blessing of all members of his family, since his brother Harold, perhaps in order to distance himself from Beorn's murder, is recorded as going to Dartmouth to exhume his cousin's body and have it more honourably buried next to that of his kinsman Cnut in the Old Minster, Winchester. The removal of Swein from England in 1047 may have encouraged Edward to consider the prudence of relying so heavily on the Godwines. And indeed, at about this time, in the mid to late 1040s, there are signs of escalating political divisions in England and of Edward's favouring of those outside the Godwine family. In 1047, as we have seen, the king had disregarded the advice of Godwine about the wars in Scandinavia, preferring instead to follow that of Earl Leofric. And in 1049 Edward had offered military support to Emperor Henry III against Count Baldwin of Flanders, the very person who had supported Swein in 1047 after his flight from England. The *Vita Ædwardi*, naturally biased in favour of Edith, Godwine's daughter, describes the emergence of one political faction, led by Robert of Jumièges, who influenced the king in making decisions and how 'through his assiduous communication with him the king began to neglect more useful advice'. The problem became such that, in the eyes of this author, 'the realm gradually became disturbed', because, when office-holders died, they were often being replaced by 'strangers' (*alienis*).[33] Such actions suggest that Edward, now that he was securely established on the throne, recognized that the Godwines had become too powerful and that the balance needed somehow to be redressed.

Between 1043 and 1050, having returned from exile in Normandy, Edward had, from a position of relative weakness, managed to secure his throne, garner the support of the leading noble family, make his own appointments to office of chosen individuals and display his martial prowess in both domestic and European spheres. Although Swein managed to regain his earldom in England in 1050, by March 1051 Edward was able to appoint Robert of Jumièges – arch-rival of the Godwines – to the archbishopric of Canterbury. Little did the king know that this appointment to ecclesiastical office presaged a dramatic clash between himself and the Godwines in 1051–2 which would bring the country to the brink of a major civil conflict.

3
A Crisis of Royal Authority

The years 1051–2 were the most critical of Edward's reign. A sequence of confrontational episodes between Edward and the Godwines led ultimately – and startlingly – to the banishment of the earl and his sons from the kingdom, only for them to force their way back to their former positions of power; Queen Edith, Godwine's daughter, was removed from favour, sent to a nunnery, and divorce proceedings considered before she, too, regained her status at Edward's side. What caused this crisis and why did the relationship between Edward and the Godwines break down so catastrophically? Contemporary sources point to two episodes in particular that caused disagreement: the appointment in 1050–51 of Robert of Jumièges as Archbishop of Canterbury and a serious disturbance at Dover in 1051 involving the king's brother-in-law, Eustace of Boulogne. Both episodes provoked strong reactions in the parties involved and it is significant that they each relate to the south-eastern part of England, an area vulnerable to invasion, and where Edward, as we will see, may have been attempting to counteract the power and influence that Godwine enjoyed as earl. But there were longer-term repercussions and wider considerations as well, including relationships between England and both secular and ecclesiastical powers in continental Europe, the legacy of events from earlier in the eleventh century, and the question of succession, which was to remain an issue throughout Edward's reign. Above all, this was an attempt by the king to assert his dominance over the leading secular family in the kingdom.

The drama of this short period elicited some of the most vivid, entertaining and partisan accounts to have survived from late Anglo-Saxon England; but there are complexities in handling this evidence, since a major source for the years 1051–2 is provided by three versions of the *Anglo-Saxon Chronicle* (C, D and E) which, for reasons of authorial bias, often differ from one another.[1] A detailed account of the clash between Edward and the Godwines is also to be found in the *Vita Ædwardi*, and, as we have seen, this too was written from a particular perspective, namely that of its patron, Queen Edith. It is self-evident that we need to be aware of these individual biases, and in what follows it will be necessary to note the differences of opinion between them.

On 29 October 1050, Eadsige, Archbishop of Canterbury, died. The *Vita* informs us that the community of Christ Church, Canterbury, elected as successor one of their own members, a monk named Æthelric, in line with canon law. Æthelric was himself related to Godwine and, because the earl wielded power in Kent, he was encouraged by the Canterbury community to commend their chosen successor directly to Edward.[2] But Edward was not willing to accept his election. At a meeting of his witan in

London in the middle of Lent 1051, he appointed instead his own man, Robert of Jumièges, who was then moved from his position as Bishop of London to be the new Archbishop of Canterbury. Spearhafoc (meaning 'Sparrowhawk'), Abbot of Abingdon, was made Bishop of London in Robert's place, and Rodulf, described by the *Anglo-Saxon Chronicle* as being related to Edward, was made Abbot of Abingdon.

There were many different motivating factors for the opposing positions of the king and the earl. The *Vita Ædwardi*, writing above all with Edith in mind, attributes most of the blame for the rejection of Æthelric, the Godwine candidate, to Jumièges himself. Robert is depicted as having an increasingly powerful and baleful influence on the king, a figure who gave bad counsel to Edward and manipulated him in order to achieve his ambitions, one of which was to become archbishop. The *Vita* records rather wearily that 'by his [i.e. Robert's] counsel many things both good and bad were done in the kingdom, with varying result, as is the way of the world'.[3] It continues by saying that, once Robert had been made archbishop, he was increasingly able to use his position of power to sway the king against the interests of Godwine. In doing so, Robert is depicted as malevolently reminding Edward of Godwine's role in the death of Alfred in 1036, and as suggesting to the king that Godwine now had similar intentions towards Edward himself.

But Edward, even if he did allow himself to be guided by Robert, clearly had his own agenda in opposing the election of Æthelric. Perhaps, primarily, there were issues of authority at stake. Edward's imposition of Robert on Canterbury

was a powerful demonstration of his sovereignty over Godwine in a part of the kingdom where Godwine had control of
local government. Not only was this symbolically important, but it may also have involved the significant consideration
of landed resources and wealth. In an aside, the *Vita
Ædwardi* allows that, if Godwine could be accused of anything negative in connection with the Canterbury church, it
was that he had encroached on the lands of the archbishopric. It is possible, therefore, that Edward was conscious of
Godwine's self-aggrandizement in the south-east at the
expense of the Church and sought a way to prevent the earl's
power from growing yet further, both by introducing his
own candidate into Canterbury and by blocking a relative of
Godwine's from being appointed.[4] In his other appointments
to ecclesiastical office of this year (Spearhafoc to London,
and Rodulf to Abingdon), Edward can be seen to have taken
a similar approach of inserting men who were intimately
connected to his own interests, Spearhafoc in having been
the king's goldsmith and Rodulf in being related to Edward.[5]

It thus appears that, by 1050–51, Edward was relying
less on Godwinist power and acting more independently
himself, drawing on a set of individuals whom he could
trust. There were also broader, European considerations.
In the mid eleventh century, Pope Leo IX had placed an
emphasis on ecclesiastical reform, pursuing in particular
the abuse of simony (the purchasing of ecclesiastical office)
and the degree of influence the nobility had in ecclesiastical matters. Edward's Church was not disconnected from
this papal drive for reform: the *Anglo-Saxon Chronicle*
records, for example, the holding of a major synod at

Rheims in 1049, at which the pope was present and to which Edward sent Bishop Duduc of Wells, Abbot Wulfric of St Augustine's, Canterbury, and Abbot Ælfwine of Ramsey 'so that they might inform the king of whatever was there decided in the interests of Christendom'.[6] It is feasible that Pope Leo's reforming agenda had been taken into account by Edward. But, if it had, Edward shows himself willing to ignore it when it suited him, one version of the *Anglo-Saxon Chronicle* recording in 1051 that he forced the election of Spearhafoc for London even though Archbishop Robert and Pope Leo had tried to prevent it.

The vivid entries in the *Anglo-Saxon Chronicle* for 1051 contain details of an event involving Edward's brother-in-law, Eustace of Boulogne. It appears that, when Eustace and his retainers had been looking for lodgings in Dover, a major altercation developed with the local townspeople, who objected to their presence. In the ensuing violence, men were killed on both sides. Version E of the *Anglo-Saxon Chronicle*, which is in many ways sympathetic to the Godwines,[7] blames Eustace and his men for what had happened, saying that they had arrived with military intent and that 'when he [i.e. Eustace] was some miles or more on this side of Dover he put on his corselet and all his companions did likewise'. Version D partly agrees, saying that they had acted 'foolishly'.[8] In the aftermath, Edward took the side of Eustace over the people of Dover, though D and E offer significantly different accounts. Version D states that Godwine was 'indignant that such things should happen in his earldom' and how, in an attempt to force Edward to hand Eustace over to them, he and his sons Swein and

Harold assembled an army and proceeded to Gloucester to threaten the king with war.[9] In contrast, E states that Eustace and his men gave Edward a 'prejudiced account of how they had fared, and the king grew very angry with the townsmen', with the result that the king ordered Godwine to carry out reprisals on those in Dover, which Godwine refused to do 'because he was reluctant to injure his own province'.[10] Manuscript E then says that Edward called for a meeting of his witan to be convened at Gloucester.

It is impossible to know the exact cause of the stand-off, whether Godwine was threatening Edward with military action unless his demands were met (as in D) or whether Edward had ordered Godwine to take action, only for that to be ignored (as in E). Whatever the case, Godwine may have resented intrusion by the king's brother-in-law into lands in Kent that were within his jurisdiction. In these years there are indications that Edward, with French support (such as the introduction of castles, a continental style of building), was increasing his authority in areas within Godwine's control. We have already seen Edward's influence over the appointment of Robert to Canterbury. And, by 1052, Godwine's sons Swein and Harold had witnessed castles being built in their earldoms in the south-west Midlands and East Anglia respectively. It may be that Godwine, in this episode involving Eustace, was attempting to resist similar developments in Dover. The Frenchmen in Edward's service (often labelled 'foreigners' in E) were made scapegoats in texts that put forward a pro-Godwine account of the events of 1051–2. Connections to the continent mattered for both parties, and Godwine's son Tostig was to be married at about this time to Judith, half-sister of Count Baldwin V of Flanders. In this context, the necessity of Edward looking to men such as Eustace for further support becomes all the more apparent, and 'foreigners' formed an easily identifiable group at court who could be blamed by contemporary chroniclers for the changed direction of Edward's politics in 1051–2.

In the face of a Godwinist force at Gloucester, Edward's reaction was to mobilize his other earls (and their troops), Leofric of the north-west Midlands, Siward of Northumbria and Ralph of the south-east Midlands. Leofric and Siward came at first with a small force of men, but, on realizing the gravity of the situation, they immediately sent for reinforcements. Version D of the *Chronicle* betrays the urgency felt in some quarters when it says that 'they all came to Gloucester to the help of the king, *though it was late*' (my italics). Version E tries once more to temper its account of the Godwines' actions, claiming that Godwine and his sons had come to Gloucester, not intending violence, but in order to ask the king for his advice and support. According to this account, the 'foreigners' made matters worse at this point by turning Edward's mind against the Godwines, who they said would betray the king: the result was that Edward would not see them and refused to engage in discussions. Matters had escalated and, on the brink of conflict, members of the witan advised that 'evil doing should cease on both sides'.[11] According to version D, there were those present who worried about the kingdom being left vulnerable to invasion if civil war erupted, and so a battle was avoided.[12] The memory of viking arrivals earlier in the eleventh century would have been at the forefront of people's minds.

Edward and his witan suggested another meeting be convened, this time at London 'at the autumnal equinox', to which Godwine and Harold were summoned but not Godwine's eldest son, Swein, who at this point, as E records, was declared to be an outlaw without any further hearing. Again, manuscripts D and E provide different versions of what followed. For D, Godwine, faced by the king and his forces at London, was not willing to attend the meeting and therefore fled in the middle of the night. The earl, together with his sons Swein and Tostig (and Tostig's wife, Judith), fled to Count Baldwin's court in Bruges, while his sons Harold and Leofwine went first to Bristol to pick up a ship prepared by Swein, and then ultimately to Ireland, where they sought the protection of King Diarmait mac Máel na mBó. From E's pro-Godwine perspective, the earl had tried much harder to make peace with Edward than D allows: Godwine is shown asking on two occasions for safe passage to talk with the king, and for an exchange of hostages to guarantee good behaviour on both sides, but on each occasion being denied such concessions by Edward. Some of Godwine's men seem to have changed side at this moment as well, moving over to the royal camp. If the *Vita Ædwardi* can be believed, Bishop Stigand of Winchester may have had a role as negotiator between the two parties. But the *Vita* also depicts the continued influence on Edward of Archbishop Robert of Jumièges, under whose direction the following stern message was delivered (via Stigand) to Godwine: 'that he could hope for the king's peace when and only when he gave him back his brother alive'.[13] In the mind of the *Vita*'s author, Edward's refusal to meet with Godwine and engage in meaningful discussions was motivated in part by the memory of his brother's death in 1036 and Godwine's involvement in it. Version E ends this part of its annal by saying that, having been refused a meeting with the king, Godwine was given five days to leave the kingdom.

Version D states that Godwine and all his sons were then outlawed in their absence by Edward and his councillors following a meeting of the witan. Since the early 1020s Godwine had occupied the most senior secular position below the king in the royal council. His pre-eminence appears to have been reflected symbolically at meetings of the witan, both by his name being inserted at the top of witness lists appended to royal documents, and possibly also in the seating arrangement of those gathered for the meetings of Edward's council. It would have been particularly galling for him (and his sons), therefore, that it was Edward and members of the witan itself who were responsible for deciding and then announcing his fall from power. This was clearly a moment of great historical significance. The author of version D comments how 'it would have seemed remarkable to everyone in England if anybody had told them that it could happen, because he [i.e. Godwine] had been exalted so high, even to the point of ruling the king and all England, and his sons were earls and the king's favourites, and his daughter was married to the king'.[14]

Edward had successfully checked the power of the Godwines. In an attempt to capture Harold before he left

England, as recorded in D, Edward sent Ealdred, Bishop of Worcester, with a force of men to intercept him, but, in saying that 'they could not – or would not', the author suggests that the king's wishes may have been neglected. The Godwines made good their escape and were, at least temporarily, removed from England. Edward was then able to make changes to earldoms and reward those who had supported him against the family. Ælfgar, son of Earl Leofric, was given the East Anglian earldom vacated by Harold, while Leofric himself may have received some of Swein's territories. A man called Odda, who was related to Edward, was given control of the south-western shires, part of what had formerly belonged to Godwine. Edward also took the opportunity of placing his own priest, a man by the name of William, to the important position of Bishop of London (thus expelling Spearhafoc).

Whereas Godwine and his sons were exiled, Godwine's daughter (and Edward's wife) Edith was taken from the royal court in 1051 and handed over to a religious community, a not uncommon fate in the Anglo-Saxon period for someone being removed from the political scene. As we might expect, the *Vita Ædwardi* tries to diminish the damage done to the reputation of its patron by saying that she was taken to the nunnery with 'royal honours and an imperial retinue'; but the very same passage alludes to the fact that Edward had brought formal divorce proceedings against the queen (even though these were subsequently suspended).[15] Had Edith's position as queen been jeopardized because of the fall of her father and her brothers, or was Edward motivated more by a wish to divorce the queen? Although it is impossible to be certain about the exact sequence of events,[16] the royal marriage, of five or six years' duration by 1051, may have been undergoing problems owing to the couple's continued childlessness. Fears at the royal court about the threat of invasion, should civil war break out, combined with recollection of the periods of disputed succession from the mid 1030s to the early 1040s, would have meant that the issue of Edward's heir was being discussed at the witan as a matter of some urgency, placing Edith in a precarious position even before the stand-off with the Godwines.

In the light of such concerns about Edward's successor, it is important to note this entry at the end of annal 1051 in version D of the *Chronicle*, following the account of Edith's removal from the court: 'Then forthwith Count William came from overseas with a great force of Frenchmen, and the king received him and as many of his companions as suited him, and let him go again.'[17] What is the significance of this entry? Can it be trusted as an accurate record of a visit by Duke William of Normandy to Edward's court, and, if so, what was discussed on this occasion? As it is possible that this part of the D manuscript was not written until a generation after 1051, perhaps from the perspective of the years after 1066, some scholars have felt that it should not be trusted and that a visit by William to England at that time could not have taken place. But, no matter when this record was first set down, the connection of the D manuscript with Bishop Ealdred (later Archbishop of York), a man who was intimately involved in the politics of the 1050s–60s and with the succession issue in particular, suggests that this record should be taken seriously as an account of William of Normandy paying a visit to Edward in England in 1051, regardless of his reasons for doing so.[18] While no information is provided about the purpose of his visit, it would have made sense for some kind of Anglo-Norman co-operation to have been discussed. Perhaps this involved the idea of William himself succeeding to the throne, perhaps Edward explored the possibility of a marriage alliance.[19] Freed from the influence of the Godwines, and mindful of the significant support he had been given by the Normans during his own extended exile, Edward had the opportunity to explore new political relationships, at the same time that the Godwines were establishing their own connections with other European rulers (via Tostig's marriage into the family of Count Baldwin of Flanders). Regardless of the exact substance of Edward's negotiations with William, it is possible that the example of his parents' marriage (of Æthelred, an Anglo-Saxon, to Emma, a Norman), which had been effected in order to prevent vikings from gaining Norman support, provided a helpful precedent for what could be achieved through a cross-Channel alliance. Two hostages from Godwine's family, Wulfnoth and Hakon, are later found under Duke William's custody in Normandy, and it is possible that the Godwines had been forced by Edward to concede them during the crisis of 1051.[20]

The D and E versions of the *Anglo-Saxon Chronicle* both begin their entries for 1052 by recording the death of Edward's mother, Emma, who had so skilfully engineered her survival across the reigns of Æthelred, Cnut, Harold

Harefoot, Harthacnut and Edward himself. Given that Emma had, at times, caused Edward numerous problems, it is significant, therefore, that Edward chose to bury her not with his father, Æthelred, at St Paul's, London, but with her second husband, Cnut, at the Old Minster in Winchester. This choice of burial site constituted a powerful demonstration of where Edward felt his mother's true sympathies had rested.

Whatever Edward's ambitions had been in 1051, they were frustrated by Godwine and his sons, who forced their way back to their former positions of power in England the following year. A number of obstacles had to be overcome, however, before the Godwines secured their return. According to version E, Godwine sailed from Bruges to England in late June 1052 and managed to avoid a defensive naval force under the control of Earls Ralph and Odda, before turning back to Bruges, possibly because of a storm. The manuscript describes how, following Godwine's withdrawal, attempts were made to assemble a naval force in London, only for it to disband after a delay in raising the men needed. This prompted the return of Godwine, who was later joined by his son Harold, who had sailed from Ireland with ships of his own. Godwine and Harold then proceeded to ravage various parts of southern England and the Isle of Wight, seizing ships and men as they went. In its description of the destruction and murder carried out by Godwine and Harold in the southern part of England, it is striking that manuscript E, usually sympathetic to the Godwines, is willing to emphasize the hostility of their actions. In their acquisition of ships and men, it is notable how easily Godwine and Harold were able to obtain resources in the south-east of England, where Godwine had previously held sway and where the crises involving the appointment of Robert and Eustace of Boulogne had taken place. On arriving at Dover, as E records, they 'seized ships for themselves and as many hostages as they wished. So they came to Sandwich and there they did exactly the same, and everywhere they were given hostages and provisions wherever they asked for them.'[21]

By 14 September of that year, the Godwines had arrived at Southwark in London; manuscripts C and D describe how they drummed up support among Londoners and, once the tide had come in, sailed up the Thames, past London Bridge, keeping to the southern bank of the river. Edward and his earls were ready to meet the threat of the Godwines, with a fleet of about fifty ships and a land force. Manuscripts C and D add that a Godwine force had meanwhile approached by land on the northern bank of the Thames and that the earl's land and river forces were therefore arranged 'as if they meant to encircle the king's ships'.[22] At this moment, with both sides arrayed for battle, Godwine and Harold sent messengers to the king asking to be returned to power. Version E contains a criticism of Edward at this point, saying that he refused their requests for such a long time that the Godwine forces became extremely angry and could only just be restrained by the earl from taking hostile action. According to versions C and D, recollecting what had happened at a similar critical juncture in 1051, certain influential members of the king's entourage, principally the longstanding Earls Leofric and Siward, and also Bishop Stigand, urged a peaceful reconciliation, once again reminding those present of the dangers of civil war and England's vulnerability to invasion. Only a day later, on 15 September, a major meeting of the witan was held outside London at which Godwine finally cleared himself and his sons of the charges that had been brought against them. In the words of manuscript E: 'the king granted the earl and his children his full friendship and full status as an earl, and all that he had had. And all the men who were with him were treated likewise. And the king gave the lady [i.e. Edith] all that she had had.'[23]

By late September 1052, Edward must have been devastated by how events had unfolded. The Godwines had engineered an extraordinary recovery. Memory of the political upheavals of the mid 1030s to early 1040s, combined with the recent experiences of viking attacks, certainly helped to smooth the path of the Godwines' return to power. But there were other reasons as well: Edward could have taken a stronger grip on the earldoms once the Godwines had been banished, for example by putting Wessex in his own hands (as Cnut had done after he conquered the kingdom); through the granting of land, he could have done more to build up a network of supporters loyal to the crown to offset the significant number of followers who could be drawn upon by the Godwines; and he could have done more to address the serious logistical problems in raising military troops when they were needed, which led to a slow and cumbersome process of recruitment that was no match for the speedy deployment of mercenary forces by the Godwines.[24]

Once back in England, Godwine himself regained his earldom of Wessex, while Harold returned to East Anglia. This meant that Earl Odda was removed from the south-western shires (and possibly compensated with territory in the south-west Midlands), while Earl Ælfgar was removed from East Anglia (though was later returned to East Anglia on Godwine's death). Godwine's son Swein died in this same year at Constantinople, having been to Jerusalem on pilgrimage (possibly to atone for his sins in killing his cousin Beorn). The pro-Edith *Vita Ædwardi* tells us that a thegn was despatched with 'royal pomp, as was right', to escort Edith back to the royal court to take her position as queen in the 'king's bed-chamber'.[25] Given that he had earlier entertained the possibility of a divorce, it seems unlikely that Edward would have been pleased by Edith's return; their childlessness would continue to be a serious problem. The Godwines' reclaiming of their elevated positions in England led to a backlash against some of those who had opposed them. The C and D versions of the *Anglo-Saxon Chronicle* record the outlawing of some Frenchmen 'who had promoted injustices and passed unjust judgments and given bad counsel in this country', while there were also those (Frenchmen) allowed to stay if Edward permitted it,[26] of whom some sought the safety of castles within England. Archbishop Robert of Jumièges of Canterbury, Bishop William of London and Bishop Ulf of Dorchester all fled overseas, seeking security on the continent (though William returned soon afterwards to his position as bishop in London). It seems likely that those who escaped following the return to power of the Godwines were those who stood to lose the most from this reversal in political fortunes. Prominent among those continental men allowed to stay was Earl Ralph, Edward's nephew, who retained the south-east Midlands and possibly also gained control of part of Herefordshire, which had been under Swein's jurisdiction.

Edward's attempted political revolution of 1051 ultimately failed. He had tried to assert his independence from the leading noble family, only to find them able to force their way back to positions of authority. Edward clearly found the events of 1051–2 hard to accept and, if the *Vita Ædwardi* is to be believed, he was angry and frustrated. The *Vita* describes how, when bringing a royal force to Southwark on 14 September 1052 to meet Godwine and his sons, Edward appeared 'of passionate temper and ... of prompt and vigorous action' and, when accepting the Godwines back a day later, as having to calm 'the boiling tumult of his mind' in order to do so.[27] The reinstatement of the Godwines had demonstrated Edward's own limitations of power and there are indications that this deeply affected his approach to kingship for the rest of his reign.

4
Rule, Decline, Succession

For the remainder of Edward's reign, the annals in the *Anglo-Saxon Chronicle* are never again as vivid in their detail as they had been for the years 1051–2. Against the entry for 1058, for example, the D chronicler is explicitly reluctant to set down a historical record: 'It is tedious to relate fully how things went.'[1] Amid the information that the annals do provide, it is striking how little attention is paid to Edward himself and his actions. They focus instead on the activities of the earls and note appointments to ecclesiastical office; there are also records in particular about disturbances on the periphery of the English kingdom, in connection with Wales and Scotland. A modern biographer of Edward, Frank Barlow, describes the years 1052–65 as 'an oasis of peace and prosperity', pointing to those parts of the *Vita Ædwardi* that make comparisons between Edward and Solomon, an Old Testament king whose reign was renowned for being peaceful.[2] And certainly there are signs of peace and prosperity, as demonstrated by timely intervention in affairs involving the rulers of Wales and Scotland, and also symbolically by the positive and powerful image of the king projected in the iconography of royal seals and coins and by an ambitious building project at Westminster overseen by Edward. But even if there were periods of calm and stability, this latter half of Edward's reign was also marked by serious and complex problems.

The return to power of Godwine and his sons was in effect a manifestation of Edward's inability to enforce his royal will. From 1052 onwards, it would have been imperative for Edward to maintain if possible the fine balance between his own wishes and the competing interests of the leading secular families, the houses of Godwine, Leofric and Siward. There was the added complication of the identity of Edward's successor. By the early 1050s, it had become clear that Edward and Edith would not themselves produce an heir. As we have seen, Edward, seeking to strengthen relations with Normandy, appears to have held discussions with William in 1051 at which it is possible that the idea of the duke becoming king was raised. But the return of the Godwines meant that, in the early to mid 1050s, any thought of William succeeding, if it had been discussed, must have evaporated. The potential rewards were therefore all the greater for those involved in high politics, both within England and without. Ultimately, the succession question found its spectacular final answer at the Battle of Hastings on 14 October 1066. But there were many oscillations in fortune before this happened, as the different interested parties jostled for position.

We would very much like to know how Edward himself dealt with these challenges. The *Vita Ædwardi* states that Edward, except for events in Northumbria in 1065, was not centrally involved in the kingdom's affairs and that instead Godwine's sons Harold and Tostig had assumed control (even if the brothers are themselves criticized at times). Edward is depicted as having turned his interests to the more enjoyable pursuit of hunting, while also devoting himself to a life of piety. But can his apparent withdrawal from politics be taken at face value? The silence of the *Anglo-Saxon Chronicle* with regard to the king at this time is striking and could be taken to reflect his disengagement from political affairs. There is evidence too, for example, that Edward had lost influence over the appointment of bishops, a reversal of the pattern seen in the first decade of his reign.[3] John of Worcester's *Chronicle* offers a different interpretation, on the other hand, suggesting that the king continued to be actively involved in governance.

At the same time that Edward recedes from view in the *Anglo-Saxon Chronicle* and the *Vita Ædwardi*, the Godwines are in the ascendant. Changes in earldoms meant that, by the late 1050s, the sons of Godwine were unrivalled in power. And, by the early 1060s, Harold himself was growing in importance, able to draw on significant landed resources that set him apart from other nobles.[4] It is possible that Edward had carefully managed his earls with the result that he was able to rely on them to a greater extent than before to conduct secular business on his behalf. But some scholars have judged that this extra power in the hands of the Godwines (particularly Harold) reflects a ceding of control by Edward rather than a deliberate delegation of authority. For George Garnett, Edward had become in effect a '*roi fainéant*', a king in name only and with limited actual power.[5] Certainly this was true by the end of his reign, for in 1065, when he had to deal with a major Northumbrian rebellion, he seems to have been unable to draw on the resources needed to pacify the rebels and his failure in this regard is said to have led directly to his deterioration in health and then his death.

The gravity of the events of 1051–2 involving the Godwines cannot be overstated. The *Vita Ædwardi*, even if it lays most of the blame for the expulsion of the Godwines at the feet of Robert of Jumièges, nevertheless indicates that Edward himself played a leading role. It must, therefore, have been publicly humiliating for Edward to have to welcome back the earl and his sons so soon after his attempt to deprive them of power. But events of 1053 worked in Edward's favour: on Easter Monday of that year, while Godwine and his sons Harold and Tostig were dining with the king at Winchester, Godwine 'suddenly sank towards the foot-stool, bereft of speech and of all his strength'.[6] Although those present thought that he might recover, it was not to be. On 15 April 1053, he died and was buried in the Old Minster, Winchester. His son Harold was given Wessex, while Harold's former position as Earl of East Anglia was transferred to Ælfgar, son of Leofric of Mercia (as it had been during Harold's exile from England in 1051–2). These appointments created a relatively even spread of authority between the three major noble powers: the house of Leofric in East Anglia (Ælfgar) and the north-west Midlands (Leofric), Siward in Northumbria and Harold in Wessex. The removal of Godwine from the scene must have temporarily afforded Edward at least some respite from his troubles.

The year 1055 saw further reorganization of the earldoms. The death of Siward, Earl of Northumbria, meant
that Edward lost an established supporter in the potentially
turbulent north of the kingdom. This would not have been
an easy position for Edward to fill. And the *Anglo-Saxon
Chronicle* hints that there may have been a power struggle
upon Siward's death. We are told that Edward's choice for
the Northumbrian earldom was Tostig, brother of Harold
and son of Godwine. But the three different versions of the
Anglo-Saxon Chronicle for this year – C, D and E – also
report that, following a meeting of the king's witan at
London, Earl Ælfgar was outlawed.[7] We are not explicitly
told the reasons why he was removed from power. The C
and D versions state that he was outlawed even though he
had committed no offence, but the E version – generally
favourable to the Godwines – offers a different explanation,
attributing his removal to having been 'charged with being
a traitor to the king and to all the people of the country'.[8]
The differing accounts in the *Anglo-Saxon Chronicle*, each
version with its own political bias, probably reflect how,
following Siward's death, there had been a challenge for the
Northumbrian earldom. Ælfgar, son of Earl Leofric of the
north-west Midlands, and himself Earl of East Anglia,
would have been all too aware of the advantage to the Godwines that Tostig's gaining of Northumbria would afford.
Ælfgar had therefore vigorously resisted his appointment,
with the result that he was excluded from politics. How
much Edward himself was involved is not made clear in the
Anglo-Saxon Chronicle: he is wholly absent from the
records in C and D and makes only a brief appearance in E,

where he is described simply as giving the earldom to Tostig. More detail is provided by the *Vita Ædwardi*, which states how Tostig's siblings Earl Harold and Queen Edith had been instrumental in securing his appointment. Edward himself is described as being in favour of Tostig 'because of the innumerable services faithfully performed'.[9]

Whatever Edward's role in events, the Godwine family seems to have seized the opportunity offered by Siward's death to take control of the earldom of Northumbria. This radically altered the political balance in England as the Godwines now took possession of large swathes of the kingdom in the south and the north and effectively encircled the house of Leofric (with Leofric in the north-west Midlands and his son, Ælfgar, who had been restored to power later in 1055, in East Anglia). Harold's own lands were expanded in 1056 following the death of Earl Odda, at which point Harold seems to have taken control of parts of Herefordshire and Gloucestershire, thus advancing Godwine interests even further. It was at about this time, in the mid to late 1050s, that a new type of coin was introduced into circulation, known as the 'Pointed Helmet' type. In the design of these coins, Edward himself is wearing a helmet rather than a crown and given a beard. Here is an image of a king girded for military action; gone is the message of 'peace' from earlier in his reign.

Between 1057 and 1065 there were yet more changes to the earldoms.[10] The *Anglo-Saxon Chronicle* records that, on 30 September 1057, Leofric, Earl of the North-West Midlands, died and was buried at Coventry. Alongside Siward, Leofric had been another longstanding and powerful earl in the kingdom, someone who had held authority from the very beginning of Edward's reign. His death meant that his son, Ælfgar, could be moved from the earldom of East Anglia, to that of the north-west Midlands. (In 1058 Ælfgar was banished from England for a second time, but managed once more to reclaim his position, as we shall see.) The *Anglo-Saxon Chronicle* for 1057 reports the death of Earl Ralph, Edward's nephew, on 21 December. Ralph's death, coupled with Ælfgar's vacating of the earldom of East Anglia, created room for new earls to be appointed and it is highly significant that two sons of Godwine, Leofwine and Gyrth, were chosen for these roles; they were in position by 1059 at the latest (and possibly by 1057/8). Between 1057 and 1065, Tostig was also able to extend his own area of control into the east Midlands. The gains of the Godwine family had thus been substantially furthered, with the result that its members had an extraordinary grasp on power, controlling much of the kingdom, including Wessex, Northumbria, East Anglia and the east and south-east Midlands. With these appointments, it is possible that Edward simply continued his approach of the 1040s, relying on established noble families, and respecting hereditary succession by members of those families to the different earldoms. But it is perhaps more likely that the steady increase of power in the Godwines' hands meant that Edward had little choice but to accept their claims. The appointment in 1061 of Waltheof, son of Siward, as earl in Northamptonshire and Huntingdonshire, and then of Eadwine, son of Ælfgar, to the north-west Midlands in 1062–3, represented isolated examples of gains by individuals outside the Godwine family.

The latter part of Edward's reign, then, saw different men being chosen as earls. The Godwine family sought to exploit every available opportunity, even if their power was, on occasion, checked by the Mercian family of Leofric. The *Vita Ædwardi* suggests that, with Harold and Tostig as Earls of Wessex and Northumbria respectively, Edward was no longer as actively involved in governing the kingdom and that he therefore 'lived all his life free from care on either flank, for the one drove back the foe from the south and the other scared them off from the north'.[11] With Harold and Tostig in charge, Edward is depicted as being able to indulge his own interests, rather than concerning himself with the business of being king.[12] It is possible that, by the late 1050s, the power of the two earls, and the rest of the Godwine family, was such that Edward's role had been diminished. From the evidence of charters and Domesday Book (as we will see in the next chapter, a major survey of landed resources conducted in 1085–6 that gives figures for the value of lands owned by different people and institutions in Edward's day), it is clear that Harold and Tostig had vast amounts of wealth on which to draw, much more so than the members of any other noble family.[13]

Whatever the realities of Edward's political position, there were attempts to create at least the image of strong kingship, as reflected in changes in the designs of the king's coins and seals. In the late 1050s, following on from the 'Pointed Helmet' type, a coin known as the 'Sovereign/ Eagles' type began to be circulated. In a fascinating, and almost unprecedented, departure from established custom, the bust of the king is replaced by a monarch enthroned in majesty, with a staff in one hand and a globe in the other. On the reverse of the coin is another unique feature: this side is divided into quarters and within each quarter is the image of a bird, possibly intended to be an eagle.[14] This representation of the 'king' – Edward – is closely mirrored in the images on the royal seal from about the same period. Again Edward is depicted enthroned, carrying a sword in one hand and a staff (topped with either a bird or a fleur-de-lis) in the other. The seal carries the legend *Sigillum Eaduuardi Anglorum Basilei* ('The Seal of Edward, King of the English'), in which the Greek term *Basileus* is intended to convey a status more elevated than simply 'king'. In fact, in the iconography of Edward's coins and seal at this stage, and in the legend used on the seal, there is a clear allusion to contemporary imperial usage, and strong links to German iconographic practice in particular.[15] We can be confident in saying that Edward wished an 'imperial' image of himself to be publicized throughout his kingdom, marking a distinct change from what had gone before.

Edward's most notable cultural achievement was his building project at Westminster, which, having been initiated at some point in the period 1042–52, must have been moving towards completion in the latter part of his reign.[16] We know that a monastery dedicated to Saint Peter, although not a major site, was already present at Westminster when Edward thought about having it entirely rebuilt. The *Vita Ædwardi* describes its location as being a 'delightful spot' and privileged because of its proximity to London (at that stage Westminster lay outside the walls of the city itself), which had long been established as a major trading emporium.[17] The *Vita* states that Edward desired to rebuild the site in order that he might use it as his own burial place; he therefore

> ordered that out of the tithes of all his revenues should be started the building of a noble artifice, worthy of the Prince of the Apostles . . . and so at the king's command the building . . . was made ready, and there was no weighing of the cost, past or future, as long as it proved worthy of, and acceptable to, God and St Peter.[18]

The *Vita Ædwardi* gives a relatively lengthy description of Edward's new church, while the Bayeux Tapestry includes a near-contemporary image of it that may bear at least a broad similarity to the building's core features.[19] Although Edward's church no longer exists, parts of its fabric have survived until today, incorporated within the current structure of Westminster Abbey, including one of the oldest surviving wooden doors in the country (known as the 'Pyx door'), which forms part of an entrance to the chapter house vestibule.[20] Massive in scale, Edward's new building was clearly intended as an architectural statement, an expression in stone of his kingship that he wished to be conveyed as a lasting legacy of his reign. It also bore close comparison with contemporary Norman buildings, particularly the abbey of Jumièges, reflecting once more the influence that Normandy, and Norman fashions, continued to have on him. By a stroke of luck, a sequence of royal documents preserves the names of three of the master masons – Teinfrith, Leofsige and Godwine – who appear to have worked on the building of the abbey. What is perhaps striking is that, even though the new church was being built in the Norman style, two of its chief masons were, from their names (Leofsige and Godwine), clearly English.[21] The physical connections with and similarities to the abbey of Jumièges have long been noted and it may be that the influence of Robert of Jumièges had guided Edward in his approach to this project.

Edward's quasi-imperial image and architectural ambitions notwithstanding, there are indications across the period 1052–65 of troubles on the fringes of the English kingdom, in Wales and Scotland, that had to be dealt with by Edward and his witan. On occasion Earl Ælfgar, attempting to improve his position domestically following his banishment in 1055, sought alliance with the Welsh in order to gain support and put pressure on English authorities. In Gruffudd ap Llywelyn, Ælfgar found a king with ambitions for greatness who could help him. Gruffudd's own power in Wales was significantly augmented by this relationship, which was itself strengthened when Gruffudd married Ælfgar's daughter, Ealdgyth, possibly in 1055. Although Gruffudd can previously be found in the *Anglo-Saxon Chronicle* joining forces with Swein (son of Godwine) in 1046, as we saw in Chapter 2, his alliance with Ælfgar meant that from 1055 he never again acted in the interests of the Godwines and instead collaborated with the house of Leofric. Significantly, the year 1055 saw a further increase in Gruffudd's power in Wales when he overcame and killed a major rival from southern Wales, Gruffudd ap Rhydderch, King of Morgannwg.[22]

The latter part of Edward's reign saw hostile interactions between these two Welsh rulers (sometimes involving Ælfgar) and the English. In 1052, for example, as recorded in the D version of the *Anglo-Saxon Chronicle*, devastation was wrought in Herefordshire by a certain 'Gruffudd' – most likely Gruffudd ap Rhydderch. We are told that he came close to Leominster in English territory and 'very many good Englishmen were killed and Frenchmen too'.[23] Then, in 1053, according to the C and D versions of the *Chronicle*, further clashes took place between the Welsh and the English, the C manuscript informing us of the murder of Englishmen by Welshmen near Westbury on Severn and the D manuscript recording the killing by the English of Rhys, brother of Gruffudd ap Rhydderch, because of the damage he had been inflicting. Rhys's head was then taken to Gloucester.[24]

The Welsh continued to play a part in English politics. After Earl Ælfgar had been outlawed in 1055, he went first to Ireland and then to Wales to seek the aid of Gruffudd ap Llywelyn to help restore him to power. Having gathered a large force of Irishmen and Welshmen, Ælfgar engaged Earl Ralph (nephew of Edward) in a battle at (or near) Hereford. The *Anglo-Saxon Chronicle* describes how Ralph and his men put up no real resistance and how, choosing to flee rather than fight, many were killed while they made their retreat. Ælfgar and his men (and Gruffudd) then returned to Hereford and burned it, along with the church there. In retaliation, the English gathered an army from all over the kingdom and went first to Gloucester, before moving into Wales.[25] In the same year, Earl Harold had an important role in the refortification and rebuilding of Hereford, constructing defences in the town; he then reasserted English authority by negotiating an agreement with Ælfgar and the Welsh, following which Ælfgar was reinstated to his earldom in England.[26] That Harold had succeeded where Ralph had failed must have struck contemporary observers, and it was shortly thereafter that Harold gained lands on the Welsh Marches, in Herefordshire and Gloucestershire, where Edward's nephew had previously been in control.

Disturbances flared up again only a year later. The death of Æthelstan, Bishop of Hereford, meant that Leofgar, a priest in the service of Earl Harold, could be selected for the role. Although Leofgar had been appointed to an ecclesiastical office, it may have been his martial abilities that made him the ideal choice for the strategically important Hereford church – on the frontier between England and Wales. He is described as putting aside his spiritual duties and turning instead to military action against Gruffudd ap Llywelyn himself, only to be killed (along with Ælfnoth the sheriff and others) in the attempt. Such was the level of unrest, laments the *Anglo-Saxon Chronicle*, that 'it is hard to describe the oppression and all the expeditions and the campaigning and the labours and the loss of men and horses that all the army of the English suffered'.[27] Eventually – at the intervention of Earls Leofric and Harold and of Ealdred, Bishop of Worcester – Gruffudd was made to swear an agreement by which he became a 'faithful underking' to Edward.[28] Whatever agreement was reached, it seems unlikely that Gruffudd intended it to be lasting, for in 1058, the *Chronicle* records, 'Earl Ælfgar was [again] banished but he came back forthwith by violence through Gruffudd's help', suggesting that the Welsh king was once more prepared to intervene in English politics on the earl's behalf.[29] An Irish text, known as the *Annals of Tigernach*, provides the further detail that Ælfgar was aided in his return to England not just by Gruffudd but also by a certain Magnus, son of Harald Hardrada, King of Norway, and his fleet of ships.[30] By 1058 the Godwines had an unprecedented hold on the English earldoms, to the extent that Ælfgar's area of influence was surrounded (and dwarfed) by that of the Godwines. Ælfgar, having been exiled for a second time, had clearly been compelled to call on any support on offer in order to recover his position.

The annals of the *Anglo-Saxon Chronicle* contain no further record of relations between the English and the Welsh until the entry for 1063. Earl Ælfgar may have died in the intervening period, to be succeeded as earl in the north-west Midlands by his son Eadwine.[31] If Ælfgar had indeed died, Harold may have felt that this was the perfect opportunity to remove the threat of Gruffudd once and for all. Harold can be found conducting a punitive raid into north Wales at Rhuddlan, which resulted in the destruction of the Welsh dwellings there, together with Welsh ships and other property. John of Worcester states that Harold's intention was to murder Gruffudd, but that Gruffudd found out and fled in time.[32] This was followed soon afterwards by a joint action by Harold and his brother Tostig, Harold sailing with a naval force from Bristol around the Welsh coast and Tostig mounting an attack by land. The *Anglo-Saxon Chronicle* then records how the

Welsh themselves killed their own king, Gruffudd, 'because of the fight he fought against Earl Harold. He was king over all the Welsh, and his head was brought to Earl Harold, and Harold brought it to the king.'[33] With Gruffudd dead, Edward is described as being able to place Wales under the control of the Welsh king's half-brothers Bleddyn ap Cynfyn and Rhiwallon on terms that were amenable to both the English king and the earl.

But clearly no agreement in Anglo-Welsh relations could be taken for granted and hostilities might be renewed at any point. Sure enough, the annal for 1065 in the *Anglo-Saxon Chronicle* describes a murderous raid led by a man called Caradog (son of Gruffudd ap Rhydderch) on Earl Harold and his men, who had been constructing a hunting lodge at Portskewett, in south-eastern Wales, to which Edward was to be invited in due course. The D version of the *Chronicle* adds elliptically: 'We do not know who first suggested this conspiracy.'[34] A conspicuous element in many of the entries in the *Chronicle* on England and Wales in this period is the lack of reference to Edward's own decisions and actions. It is possible that this reveals a feature of the latter part of Edward's reign already mentioned: his withdrawal from politics. Whatever we think about Edward himself, the authority and decisiveness demonstrated by Harold in tackling the Welsh (and Ælfgar) are notable and worth recording, given his pivotal role in the dramatic events at the end of Edward's reign.

There were important episodes involving Scotland, too, during this period. In 1054 Earl Siward of Northumbria can be found conducting a raid into Scottish territory. The then Scottish king – Macbeth (best known as the character in Shakespeare's eponymous tragedy) – was defeated, and many of his men were killed. There were losses on Siward's side as well, not least that of his own son Osbern. John of Worcester tells us that Edward had ordered Siward's raid and that 'he [i.e. Siward] set up Malcolm, son of the king of the Cumbrians, as king'.[35] It is likely that the 'Cumbrians' referred to here were from the Kingdom of Strathclyde, an area in the north-west that was distinct from England and which extended into what is now the south-west of Scotland. Why had Edward and Siward thought it important to remove Macbeth from power and to install in his place their own choice, a son of the King of the Cumbrians? It is difficult to be certain. One possibility is that Edward was honouring some sort of relationship and agreement between himself and the King of the Cumbrians; another is that reprisals were being taken by Siward (and Edward) against Macbeth for raids launched into Northumbria and/or Cumbria.[36] The success of Siward and Edward in removing Macbeth from power was, however, temporary, for he returned to the throne shortly thereafter and remained king until 1057. He was succeeded by a man called Lulach, who himself was succeeded a year later by Malcolm III of Scotland.

Following the appointment of Tostig as Earl of Northumbria in 1055, the *Vita Ædwardi* describes how the Scots, wanting to probe the strength of Tostig's grasp on the earldom, conducted frequent raids on Northumbria. But the Scots, as portrayed by the anonymous author of the *Vita*, were an 'irresolute and fickle race of men, better in woods than on the plain, and trusting more to flight than to manly boldness in battle', with the result that Tostig was able to maintain his authority without ever having to engage in open conflict. A truce was concluded and the Scots gave Edward hostages as confirmation of their accord.[37]

Constructed according to literary conventions, the *Vita*'s description of the Scots and the Scottish landscape was intended in part to diminish the Scots in comparison with the English.[38] But its account of a truce receives corroboration from a rather remarkable addition made by a rough hand in the margin of a twelfth-century Northumbrian chronicle known as the *Historia Regum* ('History of the Kings'). Against the year 1059 it baldly states that Cynesige, Archbishop of York, Æthelwine, Bishop of Durham, and Tostig, Earl of Northumbria, escorted Malcolm III, King of Scots, to meet Edward.[39] The simple details of this annal may conceal a quite significant occasion. Malcolm was here being chaperoned by the most senior officials from Northumbria to meet Edward in the heart of English territory. That Malcolm was being taken to England is suggestive of his subordinate status to Edward. A subsequent reference in the *Historia* to Malcolm being the 'sworn brother' of Tostig implies that some kind of ritualistic ceremony may have taken place on this occasion in 1059, in which Malcolm probably swore an oath to respect Edward's kingship and simultaneously made a formal agreement of friendship/brotherhood with Tostig. Despite this declaration of loyalty, however, Malcolm clearly possessed expansionist aims that could not be suppressed, for in 1061, and on several subsequent occasions, he can be found conducting raids into Northumbria.

*

One of the most pressing questions in the latter half of Edward's reign was that of his successor. The facts in outline are that, upon Edward's death on 5 January 1066, he was succeeded by Harold, son of Godwine, who was crowned the following day. On 25 September 1066 Harold, at Stamford Bridge, managed to defeat an invading force led by Harald Hardrada, King of Norway, and his own brother Tostig (who, as we will see, was exiled from England in 1065). Then, on 14 October 1066, Harold was faced with the invasion of Duke William of Normandy at Hastings and famously lost his throne. But how did these events come about? Did Edward always intend Harold, Godwine's eldest son, to succeed him, despite there being no familial connection between them (and Harold could not, therefore, be considered an ætheling)? Had William been made some promise of the throne (perhaps in 1051), only to find it revoked, with the effect that he felt justified in his invasion?

As grandson of Richard II, Duke of Normandy, William was related to Edward, since the latter's mother, Emma of Normandy, was Richard's sister. Norman sources (written after the momentous events at Hastings and thus with the aim of justifying the Norman military conquest) would have us believe that William's claim to Edward's throne was pre-eminent: that Edward had promised him the throne following the support that Edward had received during his long period in exile in his youth; that Harold had sworn an oath to William that he would recognize his claim (an oath that Harold had then broken); and that William's invasion had been sanctioned by the papacy. But, from the early 1050s until the end of Edward's reign, there is evidence to suggest that matters were much more complicated than Norman sources indicate (English sources offer very different accounts) and that various possible successors were being considered, depending on the political circumstances. The complexity of these matters has meant that Edward's intentions for his successor have become one of the most discussed and controversial aspects of all early medieval English history.

By 1053, it was clear that Edward's strenuous efforts of 1051–2 to extricate himself from reliance on the Godwines had failed and control of the earldoms was now – as we have seen – fairly evenly distributed between the house of Godwine, the house of Leofric and Siward of Northumbria. It is at about this point (around 1053–4), according to the combined testimony of the *Anglo-Saxon Chronicle* and John of Worcester's *Chronicle*, that a man from the royal line of West Saxon kings was being considered as Edward's successor. The *Anglo-Saxon Chronicle* records that, in 1054, Ealdred, Bishop of Worcester, was sent to Cologne 'on the king's business' and was there received by the German emperor, Henry III. John of Worcester's *Chronicle* adds that Ealdred was encouraging the emperor to send messengers to Hungary so that the ætheling Edward the Exile, son of Edmund Ironside (himself half-brother of Edward the Confessor), might be induced to return to England, having originally been forced into exile by King Cnut.[40] The *Anglo-Saxon Chronicle* records the return of Edward the Exile to England three years later, in 1057; John of Worcester's text yet again supplies another important piece of information, which makes it explicit that Edward 'had decided that he should be established as his heir and successor to the realm'.[41] It is possible that, with secular power in the kingdom finely balanced between the three major noble families, Edward felt that promoting an ætheling with a traditional claim to the throne was the most prudent course of action. But if Edward's policy about succession had veered towards the ætheling, it did not last long, for Edward the Exile died soon after his arrival in England. The *Anglo-Saxon Chronicle* adds rather cryptically: 'we do not know for what reason it was brought about that he was not allowed to see [the face?] of his kinsman King Edward.'[42]

With Edward the Exile's death, his son, Edgar Ætheling, was the last remaining potential successor of royal blood to Edward's throne and there are indications that his claim was being taken seriously. In the *Liber Vitae* ('Book of Life'), a Winchester manuscript, Edgar's name appears alongside those of Edward and his wife Edith: *Eadweard rex, Eadgyth regina, Eadgar clito*.[43] It seems clear from other sources that the term *clito* was intended as an Anglo-Latin rendering of the Old English 'ætheling', suggesting that, at least in the mind of the author of this Winchester list of names, Edgar was being recorded as a possible contender for the throne.[44] It has even been argued that, because the term *clito* was normally reserved for the sons of kings, its application to Edgar therefore indicates that Edward had adopted him as his heir.[45] As we will see, there were those who took up Edgar Ætheling's cause following the Battle of Hastings, and he continued to press his claim quite far into William's reign, at times supported by Malcolm III of

Scotland (Malcolm would marry Edgar's sister, Margaret) and also by Swein Estrithsson of Denmark (Swein's own claim to the throne came via the Scandinavian royal line, his uncle having been King Cnut).

Even if there were those who favoured the succession of Edgar Ætheling, the late 1050s saw even more power accrue to the Godwine family. By around 1059, four of Godwine's sons (Harold, Tostig, Gyrth and Leofwine) held earldoms in the kingdom. And it is clear that, by the closing stages of Edward's reign, Harold had developed his own aspirations to be king. That said, Norman sources preserve a remarkable counter-claim: that in about 1064, on the command of Edward, Harold undertook a journey to Normandy to confirm that William would succeed as king. The Bayeux Tapestry has a famous scene (described also in Norman texts, but differing in detail) depicting the oath that Harold is meant to have sworn to William at two shrines.[46] In the context of Harold's, and his family's, great power and influence in England by the mid 1060s, it has proved difficult to believe this Norman claim. Harold probably did make a journey to Normandy, but there is evidence to suggest that he did so in order to free members of his family (his brother Wulfnoth and his nephew Hakon) who, as we saw earlier, may have been delivered by Edward to Duke William as hostages during the crisis of 1051–2 to guarantee Godwine's good behaviour.[47] It is possible that Harold swore some kind of oath to William in an attempt to effect the release of the hostages, but no details can be ascertained.

One of the last major events of Edward's life, a rebellion

1. A 'Pacx' coin minted in London around the beginning of Edward's reign in about 1042–4 by the moneyer Wulfstan, whose name appears around the edge on the reverse.

2. By the mid to late 1050s, Edward's coinage had evolved to depict him in militaristic terms. This 'Pointed Helmet' coin was minted in Norwich.

3. In the late 1050s, the iconography of Edward's coinage takes a radical turn. Inspired by contemporary imperial usage, this 'Sovereign/Eagles' coin minted in Wallingford depicts Edward enthroned in majesty.

P REGIS CUNCTORUM REGUM REGIMINE REGUNTUR OMNIA · SUPERA · IMA · PROFUNDAQ
senab: locu pletat habunde opib; & post istud misere uite decursu facti.
disponit sceptra utriusq; regnoru est nepe dux ducu · rexq; omnium pcul dubio
dente. paginula. Igit ego EADUUARDUS optalante potentissimo deo possidens totum
meo idonco capellano EOFRICO onomate nuncapato quodda rusinulla que abince
uite sue absq; aliqua machiatie subtilius honorifice regat dno atq; potestat postq; fin
ut ante satis russie liberu abom fiscali tributo uel ut bgali · cum omnib; adserite p
ditione pontif arcisq; constructione. his itaq; nob; ispur debuimus cuq; placent
psens codicellus nre licence scriptus damnet conculcet. atq; anathematizet
autumo psumptione audaci istmetiq; diabolico contra nrm decretu hanc dor
ompotentis genitricisq; cu uidele& alme Kintaethe marie incurrat · de hinc mea
cum dathan &abyron cuq; tortuoso beelzebub principe muscaru inbaratro infe
nisi prius hic digna penitudine studuerit illoro in eo actus emdare. Anno incar
karaxata est hec kartula. gubernante pissimo angloru cateruu rege feliciter EA
Dyr sindo bal ond gr mærso. Apirse oncenge midan uppatolang. hæt ploueg on cromban scepit · sþa egt ong
tone blinden · dl· eþu pille tuydon gr pihte on sene onimus sæn þanon egt nord pihte on sa uildan dic · sþa ano lang hæn
jano holcan · op landholcan ang lang senete on blucan pean · son ond lang soute onhuidan moter harpoon · sþane
op þa punga ond lang sæne pope siuure on puse plæter scapeon · sþa nord ond lang siuuuru on ewe pupo · sþa an
siddan sud on þa uildan dic · sþa on gr pihte to þa pendanscaure · op þa saure sud ut on þasse · sþa pest be sæ
Ego EADUUARDUS rex totius anglice gentis huid donationis libate hilari animo fieri concessi.
Ego eadsinus epi ecce archi psul corroboraui.
Ego alfricus dbone censis ecce archi eps consolidaui.
Ego lisingus crydianensis ecce pontifor rogatus a rege catonio scripsi.
Ego aeluuinus eps assensu pbui.
Ego brihtuuoldus eps confirmaui.
Ego dodico eps consignaui.
Ego caldredus eps corroboraui.
Ego aelfuuinus abba noue ecce.
Ego aegeluuardus abba glestoniensis ecce.
Ego aethelstanus abba.
Ego uulfuucardus abba.
Ego goduuinus abba.

IHMENSA BENIVOLENTIA· SVB INDE QVE SIBI OBTEMPERAHTER PER SPEVERIT ET PRAE-
ns trans cœlere adregna sup̄norū gaudiorū· Qui cum solus uolūtate cūm patris
uice gn̄e anob inchoatus sic hic donationis libellus consequenter manifestabit in prae-
lice nec ne & britanniæ telluris haud modice concedendo concessus sum cuidā
uocitat̄· Dofl̄se· scilic̄· vii· mansos illīmex adarandum co tenore quo omnib; dieb;
at potestate cū cūmq; placuerit tribuendi aut erogandi· Præcepimus autem
aximis qua immodicis rebx campis pascuis praes siluisq; exceptis istis orib; cepe
nolunia stabilius adhuc quod minime est oblimon tradendū uelimus sic hic
siqui contra cunde repta fuerint libellos Siquis autē quod futurū minime
am adnihilare uel p̄nihilo ducere cēptauerit· in primis quod grauisest ira dei
incory· notatq; se obnoxiū atq; reū omnib; horis atq; momētis soloy fiacq; par silli
ic scī p caciet repere n cum dices· sed cū de decore multimodo expulsus sic anob·
xlmi· in dictione· xii· epactaq;· xviii· & concurrente· vii· scilic; bissextili anno-

[Old English boundary clauses — three lines in insular script]

dux stabilun·	Ego osgodus minister·	Ego abedperdus min̄·
dux·	Ego ælfstanus minister·	Ego pulsperdus min̄·
dux·	Ego æglafus minister·	Ego abdricus min̄·
dux·	Ego æthdmerus minister·	Ego olunngcus min̄·
nobilis·	Ego kart minister·	Ego uulfgar² min̄·
nobilis·	Ego ætsorus minister·	Ego Lahrpini min̄·
nobilis·	Ego godricus minister·	Ego uulfsige min̄·
nobilis·	Ego ælfunnus minister·	Ego þurkytl min̄·
nobilis·	Ego ulfcytel minister·	Ego tou· min̄·
nobilis·	Ego osmarus minister·	Ego abdpin min̄·
nobilis·	Ego ægulfus minister·	Ego þurstan min̄·
nobilis·	Ego godunnus minister·	Ego ælfgat min̄·
obilis·	Ego ælfricus minister·	Ego manni min̄·

4. Edward's highly-sophisticated administration used royal diplomas to grant privileges across his kingdom. In this example from 1044, Edward grants land for Dawlish in Devon to his chaplain Leofric (line 5). The scribe has listed those attesting in the lower part of the diploma.

6. This addition in the margin of the *Historia Regum*, a Northumbrian historical compilation from the twelfth century, relates how Archbishop Cynesige of York, Bishop Æthelwine of Durham and Earl Tostig of Northumbria escorted Malcolm III, King of Scots, to meet Edward in 1059.

5. In this charter of Duke Robert I of Normandy from the early 1030s, when Edward was in exile in Normandy, Edward's name, signed as 'the king', and possibly his autograph cross appear in the bottom right-hand corner of the document among the list of witnesses, added after the original drafting of the document.

7. Edward used writs to issue royal instructions to the localities. This one is addressed, as if he were speaking to them in person, to 'all my bishops and my earls and my reeves and all my thegns in the shires in which Archbishop Stigand and the community at Christ Church [Canterbury] have land'.

8. Detail of the Bayeux Tapestry – 11th century: Edward's deathbed scene, divided into two parts.

9. Detail of the Bayeux Tapestry – 11th century: Edward's body being carried into the newly rebuilt Westminster Abbey.

10. Edward the Confessor's shrine in Westminster Abbey. Originally commissioned by Henry III and completed in 1269, the shrine was despoiled in the reign of Henry VIII and then reassembled by Mary I in 1557.

[text page] 11. An image from the front of the *Encomium Emmae Reginae*, written in the early 1040s, depicts the kneeling author handing a copy of his work to Queen Emma, while her sons, Harthacnut and Edward, look on.

in Northumbria in 1065, significantly strengthened Harold's position, for it resulted in the exile of Tostig from the kingdom. From the *Anglo-Saxon Chronicle* we learn that, while Tostig was away from Northumbria in Britford (Wiltshire) with Edward, the northern thegns massed, went to York and slaughtered Tostig's 'housecarls' (his household troops) and looted his possessions. The thegns outlawed Tostig and declared that Morcar, the son of Earl Ælfgar, should be their new earl. In a display of strength, Morcar marched to Northampton, accompanied by a large gathering of men drawn from various shires, and was met there by Earl Harold, Edward's representative.[48] Harold was informed by the rebels that he should notify Edward of their wish to keep Morcar as their earl. The king acceded to the rebels' demands and Harold delivered this news and swore an oath to them, and 'renewed . . . the law of King Cnut'. Harold had thus sided with the king and the Northumbrian rebels over his brother. Tostig and his wife Judith then went into exile to the court of Count Baldwin of Flanders, who was Judith's father.[49] John of Worcester's *Chronicle* suggests that the rebels were acting out of revenge for the treacherous slaughter of various Northumbrian thegns that had been carried out on the orders of Queen Edith (Tostig's sister) and of Tostig himself. John's text also states that Tostig had 'unjustly' (*iniuste*) extracted a large tax from the Northumbrians.[50] These accounts therefore imply that the rebellion against Tostig's rule had been caused partly by his own harsh application of the law and by his greed in trying to amass riches by various means.

In discussing the same episode, the *Vita Ædwardi* offers

two quite significant additions, the first in connection with Harold, the second concerning Edward. According to the *Vita*, Edward tried three times to pacify the Northumbrian rebels rather than engaging them in violent conflict. When this ultimately failed, Edward summoned his leading men to a council to discuss what could be done. In its description of a discussion at the council, the *Vita* makes the startling claim that there were those present who accused Harold of inciting rebellion in Northumbria against his brother Tostig. Tostig himself is said to have upheld this accusation and then Harold, 'rather too generous with oaths (alas!), cleared this charge with oaths'.[51] The *Vita* continues by describing how Edward took the side of Tostig against the Northumbrians and tried to raise a force of men from throughout England to combat the rebels. But there were problems for Edward, both in gaining the support he needed and in convincing his followers to wage war on the rebels: 'some strove to calm the raging spirit of the king . . . And after they had struggled for a long time, they did not so much divert the king from his desire to march as wrongfully and against his will desert him.'[52] These extra details reveal Edward's weak position by the end of his reign, unable to rely on the support of his men.

And what of the suggestion that Harold had been involved in inciting rebellion against Tostig, with the result that the Northumbrians turned to the Mercian, Morcar, to be earl? In this connection, we should note that Harold, at some point between 1063 and 1066, took as his wife Ealdgyth, daughter of the Godwines' long-time rival the Mercian earl Ælfgar and former wife of Gruffudd ap

Llywelyn. It is possible that Harold, aware of Edward's general decline, sought to put himself in prime position to succeed, not only by seizing the opportunity to marginalize his brother from power, but also by trying to shore up an alliance with those areas of Britain that had previously proved problematic – Mercia and Wales. By 1065 Harold must have had his eyes on the throne.

The same annal of the *Anglo-Saxon Chronicle* follows its account of the rebellion against Tostig with a description of Edward's arrival at Westminster at Christmas in order to consecrate his rebuilt abbey. But the king quickly became unwell, according to the *Chronicle*, and was thus unable to attend the consecration of his church, which took place on 28 December 1065.[53] The *Vita Ædwardi*, in its first book, states that 'he bore a sickness of the mind'.[54] In the second book, which is more hagiographic in tone, there is an extended description of Edward's death which states that, while he lay unwell, the king had a vision of two exceptionally holy monks whom he had known from his days in exile in Normandy. In the vision, the monks warn Edward that great evil would fall on England and its people because of their sins in having chosen various unworthy individuals (described as 'servants of the devil') for high office, both in secular and ecclesiastical positions. The monks tell Edward: 'within a year and a day after the day of your death God has delivered all this kingdom, cursed by him, into the hands of the enemy, and devils shall come through all this land with fire and sword and the havoc of war'. Despite protestations by the dying king, the monks confirm that their prophecy will unfold as they have stated and that Edward and his people could only hope for salvation

> when a green tree, if cut down in the middle of its trunk, and the part cut off carried the space of three furlongs from the stock, shall be joined again to its trunk, by itself and without the hand of man or any sort of stake, and begin once more to push leaves and bear fruit from the old love of its uniting sap, then first can a remission of these great ills be hoped for.[55]

It is clear from the details in this vision and the way in which they are expressed that reference is being made to the cataclysmic events that transpired with the Norman conquest, and that the author must therefore be writing this part of the text in full knowledge of how things turned out after Edward had died. In discussing the prophecy further, the author comments that Edward's vision (of the green tree) was unlikely to be fulfilled: no tree, split into parts in the way described, could ever be made whole and healthy once again without some kind of intervention. The allegorical message is that, for as long as the English people would not repent, they could not hope for remission of their sins, with the result that the punishment sent from God in the form of the Norman invaders would be an enduring one.[56] This prophecy was recast by authors later in the twelfth century in a much more positive light, as we shall see in the next chapter. But, taken in its eleventh-century form, it is remarkable for its demonstration of the bleak outlook that was felt in some quarters following the end of Edward's reign.

The *Vita Ædwardi* contains a description of those who were present to hear the prophecy uttered by the dying Edward. They included Queen Edith, who was at Edward's feet, Earl Harold, Robert fitzWimarch (a high-ranking secular official), Stigand (now Archbishop of Canterbury) and a few more who are not named but whose presence was requested by Edward when he awoke.[57] The Bayeux Tapestry, thought to be near-contemporary with the *Vita*, includes a scene which relies on this literary account for its depiction of Edward as he lay on his deathbed. The scene itself is one of the few in the Tapestry to be divided into two parts, with each unfolding within the confines of the same building. In the scene in the upper part we find Edward lying in bed, his head propped up by a man who may be Robert fitzWimarch while he speaks to a noble who may be Earl Harold; there is also a woman, who may be Edith, weeping at his feet and a priest, who could be Stigand, standing on the other side of the bed.[58] The scene is framed by the inscription: *Hic Eadwardus rex in lecto alloquitur fideles* ('Here King Edward, in bed, speaks to his faithful followers'). In the lower part Edward has died, announced by the inscription *Et hic defunctus est* ('And here he is dead'); he is now being prepared for burial by two attendants while a priest, who may once again be Stigand, looks on. The compression of the scene into two parts might be an artistic device intended to convey the rapidity with which Edward's health deteriorated. The *Anglo-Saxon Chronicle*, having told us that he had become so unwell by 28 December 1065 that he was unable to attend the consecration of Westminster Abbey, then records that Edward died shortly later, on 'the eve of the Epiphany', that is on 5 January 1066, and was buried only a day later in Westminster, the abbey that he himself had rebuilt.[59] Edward had ruled England for more than twenty years.

What happened in these closing moments of Edward's life is a matter of controversy for contemporary writers and modern scholars alike. Had the dying king bequeathed the kingdom to Harold? Extant sources differ in their interpretation. In the English texts, the E version of the *Anglo-Saxon Chronicle*, which is generally favourable to the Godwines, is explicit in saying that Edward had given the kingdom to Harold: 'And Earl Harold succeeded to the realm of England, just as the king had granted it to him, and as he had been chosen to the position.'[60] Other accounts are less clear. The presentation of events in the *Vita Ædwardi*, for example, is ambiguous: Edward is described as reaching out his hand to Harold, while in the presence of Edith, and saying, 'I commend this woman and all the kingdom to your protection.'[61] Is the instruction here that Harold should simply take care of the kingdom before it passed into another's hands? Or was he straightforwardly being given the kingdom for himself? The meaning of the inscription around the relevant scene in the Bayeux Tapestry ('Here King Edward, in bed, speaks to his faithful followers'), itself based on the *Vita*, is also unclear.

One modern historian has stressed that it would have been unprecedented for Edward to have named as his successor someone not of the royal line of Cerdic. In this commentator's view, the aforementioned listing of Edgar

Ætheling in the *Liber Vitae* demonstrates that he – *not* Harold – was formally considered Edward's heir towards the end of his reign and therefore that Harold had forcefully taken the throne for himself. This interpretation may receive corroboration from the combined testimony of sources written after 1066 by Herman the Archdeacon and Hariulf of Saint-Riquier.[62] Herman provides more information about the circumstances in which the earl became king, stating that, as soon as Edward was buried, Harold was 'enthroned in the seat of royal power, cunningly seizing the throne at the Introit of the Mass'.[63] Herman's testimony is particularly compelling, given that one of his sources was Edward's own physician, Abbot Baldwin of Bury St Edmunds. Hariulf also describes Harold's seizing of the throne and adds that Harold had previously sworn an oath to the effect that he would recognize the rights of a certain 'Elfgar' to be king, in which it is likely that this is a corruption of the name 'Edgar'.[64]

Whether or not we believe that Harold had taken the throne via a coup, the Bayeux Tapestry shows the royal crown being given to him immediately after Edward's death, following which he is depicted already crowned and enthroned, holding a sceptre and orb and being acclaimed by those in attendance. The speed of his coronation on the death of Edward is symptomatic of the instability in politics at this moment, as Harold rushed to take control and legitimize his position. The *Anglo-Saxon Chronicle* ends its annal for 1065 with the gnomic statement that Harold, having been consecrated as king, 'met little quiet in it as long as he ruled the realm'.[65]

While we cannot know for certain the answer to the succession question and what Edward's final wishes were for the future of England, surviving evidence indicates that he explored different options at different times in his reign: up until 1051 he desired a son of his own by Edith; in 1051–2, childless and considering a divorce from Edith, he looked to Normandy for support (whether or not the idea of Duke William succeeding was discussed is uncertain); from around 1054 until 1057 he backed the claim of the ætheling Edward the Exile, and finally, when the Exile died, he looked to Edgar Ætheling instead. It is striking in this connection that, on Harold's death in 1066, as recorded in the D version of *Anglo-Saxon Chronicle*, there were those who chose Edgar Ætheling as his successor, 'as was his proper due'.[66]

Edward has been criticized for his handling of the succession question, with the result that he is sometimes depicted as having laid England open to invasion from Normandy. In one historian's estimation, 'he played fast and loose with the succession issue, with disastrous consequences'.[67] But perhaps Edward, in respecting the importance of the royal line of Cerdic, did his best in the very difficult situation thrust upon him by his own childlessness. The various versions of the *Anglo-Saxon Chronicle* had for the most part omitted to mention Edward during the last decade or so of his reign. But, in describing his death, the C and D versions interrupt their usual prose narrative to insert a poem in celebration of the king:

> At length he came forth in lordly array,
> Noble in goodness, pure and upright,

Edward the glorious, guarding his homeland,
Country and subjects – till on a sudden came
Death in his bitterness, bearing so dear
A lord from the earth . . .[68]

The *Anglo-Saxon Chronicle* uses verse only on certain occasions, to mark events and deaths that were particularly important. Even if Edward had in general been regarded by the *Chronicle* as less worthy of mention towards the end of his reign, he was a king who nevertheless warranted special treatment.

5
Sainthood

When Henry III was rebuilding Westminster Abbey in the mid thirteenth century, the tomb of Edward the Confessor (who had been canonized by Pope Alexander III in 1161) was placed at its heart. The abbey, and its immediate environs, became the hub of medieval English government. This transformation in Edward's symbolic importance was in part a recognition of his status as an important royal saint; it was in part also a demonstration of the affection that Henry III felt for this last king of the line of Cerdic. The centrality of both Edward's tomb and his saintly image had the result that regalia associated with him played a major role in the investiture of the monarchs of England. Any visit to Westminster Abbey today reveals the high regard in which Edward was held in the thirteenth century. Wall paintings in the Palace of Westminster, where kings and monarchs-in-waiting would have lived, slept and conducted business, illustrated principal scenes from Edward's life, combined with representations of the key virtues expected of a thirteenth-century king, *Deboneretê* and *Largesce*.[1] How did Edward achieve such prominence? This chapter examines the development of Edward's image and status in the late eleventh and twelfth centuries, how the memory of

Edward came to hold significance in both secular affairs (as William the Conqueror's predecessor and as a king associated with providing good laws) and in spiritual matters (for those at Westminster Abbey who petitioned for him to be made a saint).

In the wake of the Norman conquest, successive rulers, from William the Conqueror (d. 1087) through William Rufus (d. 1100) to Henry I (d. 1135), were faced with challenges to their legitimacy as kings of England. Norman historians in particular, writing after the momentous events of 1066, stressed that William the Conqueror had a natural and legitimate right to the English throne, both through his being related to Edward (William of Poitiers describes Edward as the 'kinsman' (*consanguineus*) of William)[2] and through the promise of the throne that had been made to him by Edward (which, they say, had originally been respected by Harold, son of Godwine, via an oath sworn to William). In asserting this claim, it was important for these Norman writers to ensure (as far as possible) that the nine-month reign of Harold was thought of as a usurpation, a brief interruption in the rightful order of succession. This had two consequences for Harold himself: that he was depicted as a perjurer and oath-breaker; and that a kind of *damnatio memoriae* took place, a removal of Harold's status as king from history. The need to treat Harold in such a manner led simultaneously to a heightened respect for the reign of Edward, who was held up as the last legitimate Anglo-Saxon king, the man who had bequeathed the throne to William, only for it to be seized by Harold.[3]

A prominent example of this omission of Harold from

the written record, and concurrently of the recognition of Edward's status, can be found in Domesday Book. In 1085–6 William the Conqueror commissioned and oversaw the compilation of a vast survey of all properties and rights across most of the country. England was divided into administrative circuits, and commissioners were sent into them to discover who owned what land and property at two points in time, both 'on the day King Edward was alive and dead' (*tempore regis Eadwardi*) and 'in the time of King William' (*tempore regis Willelmi*). The results of the survey were written down and came to be known as Domesday Book – meaning literally in Old English the 'book' (*boc*) of 'judgement' (*dom*) – a volume that was truly revolutionary in character. Its principal aim was to record the fiscal rights belonging to the king (and others) and how these had changed from the last days of Anglo-Saxon rule to those of Norman times. The omission of Harold's reign in the pages of this official record, and instead the recognition of Edward as the last Anglo-Saxon king, represented one stage in the enshrining of Edward's reign in legal memory.[4]

As well as details about estates ownership, Domesday Book reveals the profound changes that took place after the Norman conquest in terms of the aristocracy, as the English were removed en masse from their former positions of wealth and power and replaced by men from the continent. These changes brought with them complexities of co-existence, particularly in the area of law, as the English were disquieted by the deviations from their customs and legal system that were introduced by their conquerors; at the same time, the new Norman lords needed to demonstrate that their conquest had been legitimate and that they were operating according to established legal custom. In this atmosphere of uncertainty for both parties, Edward's laws gained theoretical and symbolic importance as the legal benchmark for all concerned: they represented stability and continuity for the English; meanwhile the Normans, even if making changes, could reassure their subjects that they were governing according to the *laga Eadwardi* ('the laws of Edward'), a phrase that was designed to encapsulate all pre-conquest law and custom, rather than a specific set of laws (there is no surviving law code in Edward's name from the time of his reign). Perhaps the most famous example of this occurs in the coronation charter of Henry I, dated 5 August 1100. This document, issued at the outset of Henry's reign, was designed by the king to secure the support of his subjects by detailing the principles with which he intended to rule. At various moments in the body of the document, reference is made to how things used to operate 'in the time of King Edward' or 'according to the law of King Edward'.[5] The importance of the *laga Eadwardi* was such that, by the mid twelfth century, an anonymous author composed a legal tract that gave details of these laws, entitled the *Leges Edwardi Confessoris* ('Laws of Edward the Confessor'), which became one of the most popular legal texts of its time and was copied and adjusted on many subsequent occasions.[6]

The memory of Edward and his reign was therefore important for Norman kings in framing their own rule and demonstrating that they were aspiring to act according to the precedent of Anglo-Saxon kings. How, and in

what circumstances, did Edward become a saint? The *Vita
Ædwardi* is the earliest text to give an outline of his life
and death. Although it is not a straightforwardly hagiographical work, its second book in particular imputes
some saintly aspects to Edward: it begins by stating that he
had 'lived his whole life dedicated to God in true inno-
cence' and proceeds by describing how God had 'glorified
him in this life of corruption by these signs'.[7] A small number of miracles enacted by Edward while he was still alive
are described in the *Vita*, including one involving a woman
who was suffering from scrofula – an infection of her
throat and the glands in her neck which had 'disfigured her
face with an evil-smelling disease', a malady that was later
known as the 'king's evil'.[8] It was revealed to the woman in
a dream that if King Edward were to wash her, she would
be cured of her ailment, thereby promoting the idea that
the disease could be cured by royal touch. Edward, having
heard about the woman and her dream, sought to help her
and, placing his hand in water, began to touch the affected
parts of her face and neck with his fingertips, making the
sign of the cross as he did. Sure enough, 'those diseased
parts that had been treated by the smearing of the king
softened and separated from the skin; and, with the pressure of the hand, worms together with pus and blood came
out of various holes'.[9] Edward then made sure that the
woman was housed and provided with food until she was
fully recovered from the disease. In its description of this
and other miracles, the *Vita Ædwardi* thus suggests that
signs were already emerging during Edward's lifetime of
his sanctity. It also states that these kinds of curative

miracles had been performed by Edward while in exile in Normandy; it is possible that his ability to heal people was stressed during that early part of his life in order to demonstrate his suitability for the throne, as a man specially marked by God.[10] Book two of the *Vita* concludes by saying that, following his death, a number of miracles were being performed at his tomb in Westminster, which reveals that Edward 'lives with Him as a saint in heaven'; there is evidence that his tomb later in the eleventh century also became a place of sanctuary to which criminals could flee, hoping for temporary respite from their pursuers.[11]

Later authors fastened on the saintly aspects of Edward's life. William of Malmesbury, writing his *Gesta Regum Anglorum* ('The History of the English Kings') in the early twelfth century, made use of the earlier *Vita Ædwardi* when giving details about Edward and his reign. He describes Edward's miracles, his gentle and mild manner and his moderation, suggesting that 'the simplicity of his character made him hardly fit to govern, but he was devoted to God and therefore guided by Him'.[12] William also stresses that the king seemed to have lived a celibate life, despite having been married. As a result of Edward's special connection with God, his reign was marked for its lack of civil or foreign wars, according to William, who presents Edward primarily as a peaceful king. Similar themes are discussed by other authors of the twelfth century, including Orderic Vitalis and John of Worcester.[13]

Edward's image as a saint was given added impetus by Osbert of Clare, a monk of Westminster Abbey and later its prior, who, in 1138, wrote his own *Vita* of Edward, the *Vita*

Beati Eadwardi Regis Anglorum ('The Life of Saint Edward, King of the English'), using the earlier *Vita Ædwardi* as a model. Osbert is famous not just for his *Vita* of Edward, but also for a collection of letters in his own name and for overseeing the composition of a series of charters forged in favour of Westminster Abbey. The first half of the twelfth century in general saw various ecclesiastical houses resorting to the forging or 'updating' of their archives in order to make sure that they had written proof of their assorted claims to lands and privileges. The accession of Stephen as king in 1135 had led to a period of civil war in England known as 'the Anarchy', during which law and order came under significant strain and royal authority was extensively undermined. Written proof of ownership, already important, now counted more than ever. It was against this background of general political unrest – and recognizing that Westminster Abbey had been poorly managed, to the extent that its buildings were in disrepair and many of its landed assets had been lost – that Osbert resorted to the forging of a series of documents.[14] These forgeries invoke the names of celebrated Anglo-Saxon figures, notably Saint Dunstan (d. 988) and King Edgar (d. 975). But the most famous set of documents includes the so-called First, Second and Third Charters, which each record significant benefactions made by Edward himself to Westminster Abbey and which have been judged to be spurious.[15]

In the documents forged by Osbert, many of Westminster's important lands and privileges were now listed as grants made originally by Edward in the Anglo-Saxon period. It made sense for Osbert to claim that these charters had been issued by the royal founder of the abbey. It may also help to explain why, as we will see, it became so important for Westminster to push for Edward's canonization in 1138–9. If Edward were to gain recognition as a saint, it would have been even harder for would-be defrauders of the abbey's lands and privileges to gainsay charters in his name. Passages of the forged charters share details (in terms of content and style of writing) with the *Vita* composed by Osbert, and the suggestion has been made that the charters and the *Vita* were taken by Osbert to Rome in 1139 when he petitioned Innocent II to make Edward a saint.[16]

One important episode in the enhancement of Edward's sanctity was the opening of his tomb in 1102, the earliest account of which can be found in Osbert's *Vita*. We are told that Edward's body was inspected by Abbot Gilbert Crispin and other men of standing, including Bishop Gundulf of Rochester, who all found it to be incorrupt. The same applied to everything within the tomb: Edward's body had been wrapped in a fine robe, there was a ring on his finger, he wore sandals and a crown and had a sceptre by his side, all of which showed no sign of decay. Gundulf was so moved by the wonder of finding Edward's body in this state that he attempted to remove a hair from the king's beard to preserve it as a relic. But those present decided that Edward's body should be left to rest 'virgin and incorrupt'; the tomb was therefore closed once more.[17]

Osbert's *Vita* contains descriptions of new miracles associated with Edward,[18] including the healing of a cripple, seven blind men and a blind bell-ringer, and Edward's appearance in a dream vision to Abbot Ælfwine of Ramsey.

But perhaps Osbert's most famous addition is the story of Bishop Wulfstan of Worcester and his staff. During an ecclesiastical council at Westminster, according to Osbert, Archbishop Lanfranc of Canterbury attempted to remove Wulfstan from his position. Wulfstan, replying that he would only return his bishop's staff to the man who had invested him with office – namely, Edward – thrust it into the top of Edward's tomb where it became fixed, impossible to move by all those who tried, including Gundulf of Rochester. A version of this account, written around the middle of the twelfth century by Ailred of Rievaulx, gained popularity in the early thirteenth century and was depicted in various forms, including a set of tapestries for the choir of Westminster Abbey donated by Abbot Richard of Barking.[19]

As well as describing new miracles, Osbert took care to burnish the saintly image of Edward by describing how he and his wife, Edith, had always maintained a chaste marriage (thus explaining their childlessness). The notion of Edward living according to a vow of chastity – a recognized hagiographical topos – became a particularly important element in the case for him to be canonized. Here Osbert found useful material in the earlier *Vita Ædwardi* on the relationship between Edward and Edith, but used these passages to new ends. For example, the earlier *Vita*, when describing the care taken by Edith in how Edward dressed, records how the queen was behaving 'more like a daughter than a wife, not so much a spouse as a good mother'. Likewise, when Edward is dying, he entreats God to be kind to his wife, 'for certainly she has served me devotedly, and has always stood close by my side like a beloved daughter'.[20]

Although the anonymous author was simply trying to show Edith as particularly supportive and caring of her husband, such details could be reinterpreted by Osbert as evidence of Edward having led a chaste life.

With the completion by Osbert of his new *Vita* of Edward in 1138, the time must have seemed ripe for the official petitioning of the pope to canonize him. Alberic, the papal legate, had been presented with a copy of the new *Vita* in December at the ecclesiastical council held by him at Westminster. Some time later, Osbert himself set off for the papal curia in Rome, taking with him a copy of his *Vita* and also letters from King Stephen, Bishop Henry of Winchester (the king's brother) and the chapter of St Paul's, all supporting the case for Edward to be recognized as a saint.[21] Conditions were therefore such that, in 1138–9, Osbert would have felt well placed to champion Edward in Rome itself since he had the support of various members of the royal family,[22] including Gervase of Blois, the son of King Stephen, who served as Abbot of Westminster from 1138 to around 1157.

But the opportunity did not last long. Pope Innocent II, in a letter of 9 December 1139 to Abbot Gervase and the brothers of Westminster, declared that he would have to defer any decision about Edward's sanctity because he would have expected to receive more letters of support for such an important case.[23] This may constitute only part of the reason for the pope's reluctance. In contemporary letters there are hints of divisions and difficulties within the Westminster community itself; in addition, the Austrian monk Sturm of Fulda had only recently been canonized, which may have made Innocent II less interested in this most recent petition.[24] The instability of the political situation may also have been an important consideration, for in June 1139 Stephen infringed the Church's rights by ordering the arrest of the Bishops of Salisbury and Lincoln, which led to a major disagreement with his brother Henry, Bishop of Winchester; and matters were further inflamed by the arrival in England in October of the Empress Matilda and her chief supporter, Robert of Gloucester, intent upon taking the kingdom by force and challenging Stephen for the throne. In the circumstances, it may have seemed prudent to Innocent II, in December 1139, to delay making a decision on this sensitive matter.[25]

Osbert's case was unsuccessful. But the dossier of documents he had assembled, including his own version of Edward's *Vita*, formed an important precedent for those at Westminster, and helped renew interest in Edward some twenty years later. By around 1158 Westminster had a new abbot in Lawrence, a man originally from the north of England and who had spent time studying near Paris, at the abbey of Saint-Victor. Having investigated Edward's rumoured sanctity, Lawrence and the Westminster brethren decided once more to petition Rome for Edward to be sanctified. Their timing was impeccable, for in 1159 King Henry II of England had helped to secure the election of Alexander III as pope, meaning that there was now a pontiff of the Roman see who would take their approach seriously.

In reaching his decision in 1139, Pope Innocent II had expressed surprise at the paucity of supporting material offered by the Westminster party in their petition. Abbot Lawrence was determined that this would not happen again, as demonstrated by a manuscript preserved in the Vatican Library that contains a sequence of fourteen letters concerning Edward's canonization, thirteen of which (the majority seeming to date from the summer of 1160) are addressed to Pope Alexander III, while the fourteenth is a letter from Pope Alexander to Abbot Lawrence and the Westminster chapter.[26] The thirteen letters are in the names of King Henry II himself and important churchmen such as Roger, Archbishop of York, Henry, Bishop of Winchester, and Gilbert Foliot, Bishop of Hereford, as well as various abbots. As a collection, these letters (in varying degrees of detail and emphasis) provide unanimous support for Abbot Lawrence's petition to have Edward canonized. They describe a general belief that Edward had reigned piously, that, though married, he had led a chaste life, that he had the gift of prophecy, that his body was found incorrupt many years after being buried, and that miracles had been performed at his tomb. Gilbert Foliot's letter contains reference to the currency of Edward's laws in the mid twelfth century, a theme touched upon at the beginning of this chapter. Two of the letters were written by those who had themselves witnessed miracles relating to Edward at Westminster. We gain an indication of Lawrence's own actions, for one of the letters demonstrates that he had visited Alexander's legates, Henry and Otto, in Paris, taking with him the pall in which Edward had been buried and which had itself been preserved incorrupt, as was found at the opening of Edward's tomb in 1102. The production of this relic was intended to convince the legates of the veracity and genuineness of Lawrence's petition. Duly impressed, Henry and Otto added their support to that of King Henry II and the array of ecclesiastical dignitaries who had been persuaded by Lawrence to support the Westminster cause.[27] Upon receipt of all of the evidence collected by Abbot Lawrence, and in order to repay Henry II for supporting him, Alexander III dispensed with the need for a formal council and issued a papal bull on 7 February 1161, with the result that Edward was admitted to the ranks of those known as holy confessors.

Lawrence then commissioned his kinsman Ailred of Rievaulx to rewrite the *Vita* of Edward in order to provide an authoritative account of the new saint's life and miracles. The translation of Edward's body into a new, and more fitting, tomb took place on 13 October 1163 at Westminster and was celebrated by Henry II and Archbishop Thomas Becket himself in the company of many of the major bishops, abbots and earls of the country. It is thought that Ailred used the occasion to present his *Vita* and then also preached a homily.[28] Ailred's *Vita* offered a view of Edward's life and miracles that was sensitively reconstructed to suit contemporary concerns. In its prologue, Ailred describes how England is famous for its saintly kings and how Edward is the pre-eminent example of such a monarch; he also reminds his readers that Henry II's royal dignity and authority stem partly from the fact that he is a direct descendant of Edward's line. Edward is here being connected to the Plantagenet dynasty, lending it legitimacy and authority. When the anonymous author of the eleventh-century *Vita Ædwardi* described Edward on his deathbed, we saw that the Anglo-Saxon king was said to have experienced a vision in which two monks revealed to him how God's punishment (manifested in the form of the Normans) would wreak havoc upon the English people for their evils and iniquities. For this eleventh-century commentator, the Norman conquest had irreparably interrupted the line of English kings (represented by the severing of a green tree) and was causing indescribable damage to the kingdom, a destruction that could not be undone. But for Ailred, writing in the 1160s, this prophecy was no longer doom-laden. In fact, as he explains, the tree (representing the English kingdom) could grow again from its roots and it did so when King Henry I (of Norman blood) married Matilda, who was the great-granddaughter of Edmund Ironside, an Anglo-Saxon king and Edward's brother. The tree then flowered when Henry I and Matilda gave birth to a daughter, the Empress Matilda, and finally it once more bore fruit when Henry II 'rose from it like the morning star, joining the two peoples like a cornerstone'. In Ailred's retelling of the original prophecy, Henry II emerges as the only person who could unite the English and Norman peoples and bring harmony to the kingdom: 'now certainly England has a king from English stock'.[29]

In the mid twelfth century, Henry II's status and prestige were augmented by the link created with the old line of English kings and the Plantagenet dynasty was strengthened; his support for the cult of Edward at Westminster helped to legitimize his position. The gathering at Westminster on 13 October 1163 was significant for another reason: Henry II had attempted to assert ancient royal rights over those of the Church, thus affirming and worsening the quarrel with Thomas Becket that would result in the dramatic martyrdom of the archbishop in 1170.[30] Viewed in the light of this disagreement, the translation of Edward's body had clearly also been intended as a demonstration of the sanctity of kingship and the inviolability of Henry's position.[31] The cult of Edward was never widely popular. But the advantages for a king of England in harnessing the memory of this Anglo-Saxon king (now also a saint) were to be recognized again a century later: for in the mid thirteenth century King Henry III rebuilt Westminster Abbey in the supreme style of Gothic architecture that can still be seen today. And by 1269 a glorious shrine had been completed as the centrepiece of the new abbey into which Edward's body was translated, carried by Henry III himself.[32] The legacy of Edward – a survivor of political exile in his early life and of manifold other vicissitudes when king – persists, commemorated at the centre of one of the most important buildings in the country.

* * *

By any measure, Edward's reign constituted an extraordinary period in British history. The question of succession upon his death, leading ultimately to the events of 1066, means that he is forever imprinted on our historical consciousness. And his burial in Westminster Abbey, and the continued use of relics connected to Edward in the crowning of our monarchs, means that his importance as a figurehead of English monarchy endures.

We can reconstruct in varying detail the different stages of his life: from his position as a child sent into exile in Normandy, through the beginnings of his reign amid difficult domestic politics, to the crisis of royal authority in 1051–2 and his retreat from politics in the last decade or so of his life. One would dearly like to know more about Edward the individual. What was his personality like? What did he look like? Our sources do not permit such questions to be answered with any degree of certainty. At the beginning of its account, the *Vita Ædwardi* gives a stylized description of Edward as

> a very proper figure of a man – of outstanding height, and distinguished by his milky white hair and beard, full of face and rosy cheeks, thin white hands, and long translucent fingers; in all the rest of his body he was an unblemished royal person. Pleasant, but always dignified, he walked with eyes downcast, most graciously affable to one and all. If some cause aroused his temper, he seemed as terrible as a lion, but he never revealed his anger by railing. To all petitioners he would either grant graciously or graciously deny, so that his gracious denial seemed the highest generosity. In public he carried himself as a true king and lord; in private with his courtiers as one of them, but with royal dignity unimpaired ... This goodly king abrogated bad laws, with his *witan* established good ones, and filled with joy all that Britain over which by the grace of God and hereditary right he ruled.[33]

This conventional description of a king cannot be taken literally. Nor can the depiction of Edward on his coins and seal, or in the Bayeux Tapestry. But there is another image of Edward at the front of a mid-eleventh-century manuscript held at the British Library.[34] The manuscript itself preserves a copy of the *Encomium Emmae Reginae*, written in the early 1040s before Edward had risen to the heights of his power. And there, as the frontispiece to the text, is an image showing Emma enthroned and receiving a copy of the work from the kneeling author, while her two sons – Harthacnut and Edward – peer in from the margins. Here is Edward marginalized from power and on the periphery of the English throne; he had a great deal of ground to cover before he himself could occupy the centre stage. That he managed to gain the crown and then hold on to it for such a long period of time is indicative of the skill with which he navigated the endlessly complex politics of eleventh-century England. Edward was above all a political pragmatist and it is fitting that his memory has persisted at the heart of English politics to this very day, his tomb a stone's throw from the Houses of Parliament.

Notes

ABBREVIATIONS

ANS — *Anglo-Norman Studies* (journal)

ASC — *The Anglo-Saxon Chronicle: A Revised Translation*, ed. D. Whitelock, D. C. Douglas and S. I. Tucker (London: Eyre and Spottiswoode, 1961); cited by manuscript and annal, and, where the original entry is incorrectly dated in the manuscript, correct date supplied in brackets

ASE — *Anglo-Saxon England* (journal)

Barlow, *Edward* — F. Barlow, *Edward the Confessor*, 2nd edn (New Haven, CT, and London: Yale University Press, 1997; original edition published in 1970)

EER — *Encomium Emmae Reginae*, ed. A. Campbell with a supplementary introduction by S. Keynes, Camden Classic Reprints 4 (Cambridge: Cambridge University Press, 1998)

EHR — *English Historical Review* (journal)

Garnett — G. Garnett, 'Conquered England, 1066–1215', in *The Oxford Illustrated History of Medieval England*, ed. N. Saul (Oxford: Oxford University Press, 1997), pp. 61–101

JW — John of Worcester, *The Chronicle of John of Worcester*, vol. 2: *The Annals from 450 to 1066*, ed. R. R. Darlington and P. McGurk, trans. J. Bray and P. McGurk (Oxford: Oxford University Press, 1995); cited by annal and by page number in the modern edition

Mortimer, *Edward* — R. Mortimer (ed.), *Edward the Confessor: The Man and the Legend* (Woodbridge: Boydell & Brewer, 2009)

ODNB — *Oxford Dictionary of National Biography*

Stafford, *Emma* — P. Stafford, *Queen Emma & Queen Edith: Queenship and Women's Power in Eleventh-Century England* (Oxford: Blackwell, 1997)

VÆdR — *Vita Ædwardi Regis*; text and translation in *The Life of King Edward the Confessor Who Rests at Westminster*, ed. and trans. F. Barlow, 2nd edn (Oxford: Oxford University Press, 1992; original edition published in 1962)

WJ — William of Jumièges, *The Gesta Normannorum Ducum of William of Jumièges, Orderic Vitalis, and Robert of Torigni*, ed. and trans. E. M. C. van Houts, 2 vols (Oxford: Oxford University Press, 1992–5)

WP — William of Poitiers, *The Gesta Guillelmi of William of Poitiers*, ed. and trans. R. H. C. Davis and M. Chibnall (Oxford: Oxford University Press, 1998)

INTRODUCTION

1. S. Keynes, 'Regenbald the Chancellor (*sic*)', *ANS*, 10 (1988), pp. 185–222.
2. The exact limits and functions of Anglo-Saxon administrative institutions are much debated by scholars. For an overview, and one of the more positive interpretations of the extent of the Anglo-Saxon 'state', see J. Campbell, *The Anglo-Saxon State* (London: Hambledon and London, 2000).
3. See also R. Abels, 'English Logistics and Military Administration, 871–1066: The Impact of the Viking Wars', in *Military Aspects of Scandinavian Society in a European Perspective AD 1–1300*, ed. A. N. Jørgensen and B. L. Clausen (Copenhagen: Publications from the National Museum, 1997), pp. 257–65. For Edward's itinerary during his reign, see D. Hill, *An Atlas of Anglo-Saxon England* (Oxford: Basil Blackwell, 1981), map no. 169.
4. *ASC* C 1046.
5. *ASC* C 1044 and E 1043 (= 1044).

A NOTE ON THE *ANGLO-SAXON CHRONICLE*

1. For a full discussion of such matters, where it is suggested that the rivalries of the families of Leofric and Godwine prompted the differences seen in versions C and E, see S. Baxter, 'MS C of the Anglo-Saxon Chronicle and the Politics of Mid-Eleventh-Century England', *EHR*, 122 (2007), pp. 1189–1227 (at p. 1190, n. 9, for the suggestion that there may have been a version of the E manuscript at St Augustine's, Canterbury, beyond 1063).

I. CHILDHOOD AND EXILE

1. *ASC* CDE 1000.
2. F. E. Harmer, *Anglo-Saxon Writs* (Manchester: Manchester University Press, 1952), nos 103–4, with discussion on pp. 334–7 (and see Barlow, *Edward*, p. 29, where the work of Harmer is similarly cited).
3. *VÆdR* I.1 (pp. 12–13).
4. S. Keynes, 'The Cult of King Edward the Martyr during the Reign of King Æthelred the Unready', in *Gender and Historiography: Studies in the Earlier Middle Ages in Honour of Pauline Stafford*, ed. J. L. Nelson, S. Reynolds and S. M. Johns (London: Institute of Historical Research, 2012), pp. 115–25.
5. *ASC* CDE 1012.
6. J. Fairweather, *Liber Eliensis: A History of the Isle of Ely from the Seventh Century to the Twelfth* (Woodbridge: Boydell & Brewer, 2005), p. 191.
7. S. Keynes, 'Edward the Ætheling (*c.*1005–16)', in Mortimer, *Edward*, pp. 41–62 (at p. 48). Stafford, *Emma*, p. 222, makes the interesting suggestion in connection with Edward's purported time at Ely that he may have been sent there so that his political importance was diminished.
8. Harmer, *Anglo-Saxon Writs*, no. 93; although the writ itself is of doubtful authenticity, Harmer judges the detail about Edward's foster-mother unlikely to have been invented by a forger (see her discussion on pp. 303–4).

9. *ASC* CDE 1013.
10. Ibid.
11. *ASC* CDE 1014.
12. Ibid.
13. *ASC* CDE 1016. By this stage Edmund's two elder brothers, Æthelstan and Ecgberht, had already died.
14. *ASC* CDE 1016.
15. JW 1017 (pp. 502–3).
16. For a full discussion of this document, see S. Keynes, 'The Æthelings in Normandy', *ANS*, 13 (1991), pp. 173–205. For Edward's early life, see Keynes, 'Edward the Ætheling', pp. 41–62.
17. For a fascinating account of Emma's life, see Stafford, *Emma*.
18. *EER* II.16 (pp. 32–3).
19. E. M. C. van Houts, 'Historiography and Hagiography at Saint-Wandrille: The "Inventio et Miracula Sancti Vulfranni"', *ANS*, 12 (1989), pp. 233–51.
20. See WP and WJ.
21. WJ VII.5(8) (pp. 104–5).
22. Keynes, 'The Æthelings in Normandy', pp. 188–90.
23. WJ VI.9(10) (pp. 76–7). The charter described previously, in which Edward signs with an autograph cross, is undated but belongs to about this time and in association with a group of four documents all linked to the gathering of this Norman fleet and its expedition: Keynes, 'The Æthelings in Normandy', pp. 187–94.
24. Stafford, *Emma*, pp. 234–5, suggests that Robert's support for the æthelings was intended to impress Henry I of France, who was then an exile in Normandy.
25. *ASC* EF 1035.
26. *ASC* CD 1035.
27. WJ VII.5(8)–6(9) (pp. 104–7) and WP I.2 (pp. 2–5). For a full discussion of these events, see S. Keynes, 'Supplementary Introduction', in *EER*, pp. xxx–xxxiv.
28. *ASC* CD 1036.
29. *ASC* CD 1037.
30. *EER* III.8 (pp. 48–9).
31. *ASC* CD 1040.
32. Ibid.
33. JW 1040 (pp. 530–33).
34. *ASC* CD 1040.
35. JW 1040 (pp. 530–33).
36. *EER* III.3–4 (pp. 40–43); and see Stafford, *Emma*, p. 240.
37. *ASC* CD 1041.
38. *EER* III.14 (pp. 52–3).
39. E. Tyler, *England in Europe: English Royal Women and Literary Patronage, c.1000–c.1150* (Toronto: University of Toronto Press, 2017), pp. 60–61.
40. For this passage of text, and discussion of its significance, see J. R. Maddicott, 'Edward the Confessor's Return to England in 1041', *EHR*, 119 (2004), pp. 650–66. The place name *Hursteshevet* is here left italicized and thus how it appears in the original Latin of the text, because of the difficulties scholars have had in identifying its modern equivalent. In his discussion, Maddicott suggests that this could be a reference to Hurst Head, a promontory of land just to the west of Southampton Water and opposite the Isle of Wight (see ibid., pp. 659–63).
41. *ASC* CD 1042 and JW 1042 (pp. 532–5).

42. *ASC* CD 1042.
43. S. Keynes and R. Love, 'Earl Godwine's Ship', *ASE*, 38 (2009), pp. 185–223 (at p. 196).

2. ACCESSION AND POWER

1. *ASC* E 1042 and CD 1043.
2. JW 1042 (pp. 534–5), describes the importance of Earl Godwine and Bishop Lyfing of Worcester in securing Edward's accession.
3. Barlow, *Edward*, pp. 50–51.
4. Ibid., pp. 60 and 62.
5. M. Clayton, 'The Old English *Promissio Regis*', *ASE*, 37 (2008), pp. 91–150 (with text at p. 149).
6. R. Naismith, *Medieval European Coinage with a Catalogue of the Coins in the Fitzwilliam Museum, Cambridge*, vol. 8: *Britain and Ireland c.400–1066* (Cambridge: Cambridge University Press, 2017), pp. 225 and 271.
7. *ASC* C 1043.
8. F. Barlow, 'Two Notes: Cnut's Second Pilgrimage and Queen Emma's Disgrace in 1043', *EHR*, 73 (1958), pp. 649–56, and Stafford, *Emma*, p. 251.
9. *ASC* D 1043.
10. F. Barlow, *The Godwins: The Rise and Fall of a Noble Dynasty* (London: Longman, 2002), p. 34.
11. H. Summerson, 'Tudor Antiquaries and the *Vita Ædwardi Regis*', *ASE*, 38 (2009), pp. 157–84 (text at p. 172).
12. Keynes and Love, 'Earl Godwine's Ship'. For a new reading and understanding of the *Vita*, see Tyler, *England in Europe*, pp. 135–259 (at pp. 149–60 for interpretation of Godwine's gift of the ship to Edward).
13. *ASC* C 1044 and E 1045.
14. *VÆdR* I.2 (pp. 22–3), and see pp. xxxix–xliv of that edition for an explanation of Barlow's reconstruction of this missing part of text.
15. Ibid. (pp. 24–5).
16. *VÆdR* I.3 (pp. 28–9).
17. Barlow, *Edward*, pp. 50–51 and 75, and C. P. Lewis, 'The French in England before the Norman Conquest', *ANS*, 17 (1995), pp. 123–41.
18. *ASC* D 1044 and C 1046 (D 1047 and E 1044).
19. *ASC* C 1049 (D 1050 (= 1049)).
20. *ASC* C 1044 (E 1043 (= 1044)).
21. Ibid.
22. *ASC* D 1045 (= 1044) and JW 1044 (pp. 540–41).
23. *VÆdR* I.1 (pp. 16–19).
24. Edward's sister, Godgifu, had first married Drogo of Mantes (see Chapter 1) but, on his death, she then married Eustace II, Count of Boulogne.
25. *ASC* C 1045.
26. *ASC* D 1045.
27. JW 1047 (pp. 544–5) and cf. *ASC* D 1047. For the difficulties involved in using these sources, see P. Stafford, *Unification and Conquest: A Political and Social History of England in the Tenth and Eleventh Centuries* (London and New York: Arnold, 1989), pp. 84–5.
28. *ASC* E 1046 (= 1048).

29. *ASC* C 1049 (D 1050) and JW 1049 (pp. 548–9).
30. *ASC* C 1046.
31. See *ASC* C 1046, E 1045 (= 1047) and D 1050 (= 1049).
32. *ASC* C 1049. Manuscript copies C, D and E of the *Anglo-Saxon Chronicle* all give slightly different details about these events; see 'A Note on the *Anglo-Saxon Chronicle*', p. xv.
33. *VÆdR* I.3 (pp. 30–31).

3. A CRISIS OF ROYAL AUTHORITY

1. See 'A Note on the *Anglo-Saxon Chronicle*', p. xv.
2. *VÆdR* I.3 (pp. 28–31).
3. Ibid. (pp. 28–35, at pp. 28–9 for the quotation).
4. Ibid. (pp. 32–3).
5. A. Williams, *Kingship and Government in Pre-Conquest England, c.500–1066* (Basingstoke: Macmillan Press, 1999), p. 139, and see further J. Hudson, *Historia Ecclesie Abbendonensis: The History of the Church of Abingdon*, vol. 1 (Oxford: Oxford University Press, 2007), pp. ciii–cv (and pp. 196–9).
6. *ASC* E 1046 (=1049); see further Stafford, *Unification and Conquest*, p. 90.
7. The different accounts in the different versions of the *Anglo-Saxon Chronicle* are very usefully discussed in R. Mortimer, 'Edward the Confessor: The Man and the Legend', in Mortimer, *Edward*, pp. 1–40 (at pp. 8–12), to which I am indebted for this chapter.
8. *ASC* E 1048 (= 1051) and D 1052 (= 1051).
9. *ASC* D 1052 (= 1051).
10. *ASC* E 1048 (= 1051).
11. Ibid.
12. *ASC* D 1052 (= 1051).
13. *VÆdR* I.3 (pp. 36–7).
14. *ASC* D 1052 (= 1051).
15. *VÆdR* I.3 (pp. 36–7).
16. For a full discussion of such issues, see Stafford, *Emma*, pp. 263–5.
17. *ASC* D 1052 (= 1051).
18. S. Baxter, 'Edward the Confessor and the Succession Question', in Mortimer, *Edward*, pp. 77–118 (at pp. 90–95, where the disputed date of composition for the D manuscript is fully discussed).
19. See T. Licence, 'Edward the Confessor and the Succession Question: A Fresh Look at the Sources', *ANS*, 39 (2017), pp. 113–27 (especially pp. 117–19 for discussion of the different possibilities considered in 1051).
20. Barlow, *Edward*, pp. 111–13 and Appendix B.
21. *ASC* E 1052.
22. *ASC* CD 1052.
23. *ASC* E 1052.
24. For the reasons for Edward's ultimate failure against the Godwines, see Mortimer, 'Edward the Confessor', pp. 26–9.
25. *VÆdR* I.4 (pp. 44–5).
26. *ASC* CD 1052.
27. *VÆdR* I.4 (pp. 42–5).

4. RULE, DECLINE, SUCCESSION

1. *ASC* D 1058.
2. The quotation can be found in F. Barlow, 'Edward [St Edward; *known as* Edward the Confessor]', in *ODNB*; and see also Barlow, *Edward*, p. 213.
3. M. Frances Smith, 'The Preferment of Royal Clerks in the Reign of Edward the Confessor', *Haskins Society Journal*, 9 (1997), pp. 159–73.
4. P. A. Clarke, *The English Nobility under Edward the Confessor* (Oxford: Clarendon Press, 1994), pp. 13–30.
5. Garnett, p. 67.
6. *ASC* C 1053.
7. *ASC* CDE 1055.
8. *ASC* E 1055.
9. *VÆdR* I.5 (pp. 48–9).
10. Twelve very useful maps relating to the earldoms can be found in Baxter, 'Edward the Confessor and the Succession Question', pp. 77–118 (between pp. 116–17); see also the maps at the front of the current volume.
11. *VÆdR* I.5 (pp. 50–51).
12. *VÆdR* I.6 (pp. 60–63).
13. For the wealth of the Godwines relative to Edward himself, see the contrasting accounts of R. Fleming, 'Domesday Estates of the King and the Godwines: A Study in Late Saxon Politics', *Speculum*, 58 (1983), pp. 987–1007, and J. Grassi, 'The Lands and Revenues of Edward the Confessor', *EHR*, 117 (2002), pp. 251–83.
14. Scholars had previously suggested they could be martlets: Naismith, *Medieval European Coinage*, vol. 8, p. 274. For Edward's projected image as king and its dissonance with reality, see C. E. Karkov, *The Ruler Portraits of Anglo-Saxon England* (Woodbridge: Boydell & Brewer, 2004), pp. 157–73.
15. See B. Bedos-Rezak, 'The King Enthroned, a New Theme in Anglo-Saxon Royal Econography: The Seal of Edward the Confessor and its Political Implications', in *Kings and Kingship*, Acta, vol. 11, ed. J. Rosenthal (Binghamton, NY: State University of New York, 1984), pp. 53–88, and L. Jones, 'From *Anglorum Basileus* to Norman Saint: The Transformation of Edward the Confessor', *Haskins Society Journal*, 12 (2002), pp. 99–120. For further connections between England and Germany in this period, see S. Keynes, 'Giso, Bishop of Wells (1061–88)', *ANS*, 19 (1996), pp. 203–71.
16. E. Fernie, 'Edward the Confessor's Westminster Abbey', in Mortimer, *Edward*, pp. 139–50; and D. Cannadine (ed.), *Westminster Abbey: A Church in History* (New Haven, CT, and London: Yale University Press, 2019). For the literary culture of Edward's reign, see E. Tyler, 'German Imperial Bishops and Anglo-Saxon Literary Culture on the Eve of the Conquest: *The Cambridge Songs* and Leofric's Exeter Book', in *Latinity and Identity in Anglo-Saxon Literature*, ed. R. Stephenson and E. V. Thornbury (Toronto: University of Toronto, 2016), pp. 177–201.
17. For London in the Anglo-Saxon period, see R. Naismith, *Citadel of the Saxons: The Rise of Early London* (London: I. B. Tauris, 2019).
18. *VÆdR* I.6 (pp. 66–71).
19. R. Gem, 'The Romanesque Rebuilding of Westminster Abbey', *ANS*, 3 (1980), pp. 33–60.

20. W. Rodwell, D. Miles, D. Hamilton and M. Bridge, 'The Dating of the Pyx Door', *English Heritage Historical Review*, 1 (2006), pp. 24–7, and W. Rodwell, 'New Glimpses of Edward the Confessor's Abbey at Westminster', in Mortimer, *Edward*, pp. 151–67 (at pp. 163–6).

21. Gem, 'The Romanesque Rebuilding', p. 39.

22. T. M. Charles-Edwards, *Wales and the Britons, 350–1064* (Oxford: Oxford University Press, 2013), pp. 561–9.

23. *ASC* D 1052.

24. *ASC* CD 1053.

25. *ASC* CDE 1055.

26. For Ælfgar and the Welsh, see K. L. Maund, 'The Welsh Alliances of Earl Ælfgar of Mercia and his Family in the Mid-Eleventh Century', *ANS*, 11 (1988), pp. 181–90.

27. *ASC* C 1056.

28. Ibid.

29. *ASC* D 1058.

30. Charles-Edwards, *Wales and the Britons*, p. 566.

31. Available sources do not provide precise dates for Ælfgar's death and Eadwine's succession; B. T. Hudson, 'The Destruction of Gruffudd ap Llywelyn', *Welsh History Review*, 15 (1990–91), pp. 331–50 (at p.339), suggests that Ælfgar may have died in 1063.

32. JW 1063 (pp. 592–3).

33. *ASC* D 1063. For the date of Gruffudd's death, see Hudson, 'Destruction of Gruffudd'; I am grateful to Tom Licence for this reference.

34. *ASC* D 1065.

35. JW 1054 (pp. 574–5).

36. A. Woolf, *From Pictland to Alba, 789–1070* (Edinburgh: Edinburgh University Press, 2007), pp. 262–3.

37. *VÆdR* I.6 (pp. 66–7).

38. For the characterization of peoples (including the Scots) as 'barbarians' in twelfth-century English historical writing, see J. Gillingham, 'The Context and Purposes of Geoffrey of Monmouth's *History of the Kings of Britain*', *ANS*, 13 (1991), pp. 99–118, reprinted in his *The English in the Twelfth Century: Imperialism, National Identity and Political Values* (Woodbridge: Boydell & Brewer, 2000).

39. *Historia Regum* 1059, in *Symeonis Monachi Opera Omnia*, ed. T. Arnold, 2 vols (London: Longman, 1882–5), vol. 2, p. 174.

40. *ASC* D 1054 and JW 1054 (pp. 574–7).

41. *ASC* DE 1057 and JW 1057 (pp. 582–3).

42. *ASC* D 1057. A noun seems to have been accidentally omitted from part of this sentence and the modern translator has suggested inserting 'the face' as one solution.

43. This entry can be found on folio 29r of that manuscript.

44. The significance of this record is discussed, for example, by: Garnett; Baxter, 'Edward the Confessor and the Succession Question', pp. 99–100; and Licence, 'Edward the Confessor and the Succession Question'. There is a vast literature about the question of Edward's successor.

45. Licence, 'Edward the Confessor and the Succession Question', p. 119.

46. F. Stenton (ed.), *The Bayeux Tapestry: A Comprehensive Survey*, 2nd edn (London: Phaidon Press, 1965), plate 29.

47. Baxter, 'Edward the Confessor and the Succession Question', pp. 87–9.

48. *ASC* C 1065 adds that there was a subsequent meeting at Oxford (which is not recorded in the D and E versions).

49. *ASC* CDE 1065.

50. JW 1065 (pp. 596–9; at pp. 598–9 for the quotation).

51. *VÆdR* I.7 (pp. 74–83; at pp. 80–81 for the quotation); Barlow's translation is very slightly altered on the basis of important observations by T. Licence, 'The Date and Authorship of the *Vita Ædwardi Regis*', *ASE*, 44 (2015), pp. 259–85 (at p. 264).

52. *VÆdR* I.7 (pp. 80–81).

53. *ASC* CD 1065.

54. *VÆdR* I.7 (pp. 80–81).

55. *VÆdR* II.11 (pp. 116–19).

56. Ibid. (pp. 120–23).

57. Ibid. (pp. 118–19).

58. Stenton, *Bayeux Tapestry*, plate 33. In the following scene in the Bayeux Tapestry, Stigand is explicitly named and is depicted clean shaven; in the scene of Edward's deathbed, the priest (who is perhaps to be identified as Stigand) has a beard.

59. *ASC* CD 1065. The *Vita* suggests that Edward died a day earlier, on 4 January.

60. *ASC* E 1066.

61. *VÆdR* II.11 (pp. 122–3).

62. For these arguments, see Licence, 'Edward the Confessor and the Succession Question'; on the importance of Herman's work in this connection, see also Garnett, p. 68.

63. T. Licence (ed. and trans.), *Herman the Archdeacon and Goscelin of Saint-Bertin: Miracles of St Edmund* (Oxford: Oxford University Press, 2014), pp. 62–3.

64. Licence, 'Edward the Confessor and the Succession Question', pp. 123–4.

65. *ASC* CD 1065.

66. *ASC* D 1066.

67. Baxter, 'Edward the Confessor and the Succession Question', p. 115.

68. *ASC* CD 1065.

5. SAINTHOOD

1. For these details, see P. Binski, *Westminster Abbey and the Plantagenets: Kingship and the Presentation of Power 1200–1400* (New Haven, CT, and London: Yale University Press, 1995), and D. A. Carpenter, 'King Henry III and St Edward the Confessor: The Origins of the Cult', *EHR*, 122 (2007), pp. 865–91.

2. WP II.12 (pp. 120–21).

3. Garnett, pp. 71–3.

4. H. Loyn, 'Harold, Son of Godwin', in his *Society and Peoples: Studies in the History of England and Wales, c.600–1200* (London: University of London, 1992), pp. 299–321.

5. W. Stubbs, *Select Charters and other Illustrations of English Constitutional History from the Earliest Times to the Reign of Edward the First*, 9th edn (Oxford: Oxford University Press, 1913), pp. 116–19.

6. For a fascinating discussion of the complex interaction of English and Norman laws and customs, the *laga Eadwardi* and the *Leges Edwardi Confessoris*, see

B. R. O'Brien, *God's Peace and King's Peace: The Laws of Edward the Confessor* (Philadelphia: University of Pennsylvania Press, 1999).

7. *VÆdR* II.1 (pp. 92–3).

8. *VÆdR* II.2 (pp. 92–3); F. Barlow, 'The King's Evil', *EHR*, 95 (1980), pp. 3–27.

9. *VÆdR* II.2 (pp. 92–3).

10. Ibid. (pp. 94–5); for discussion of these miracles performed in Normandy, see E. van Houts, 'Edward and Normandy', in Mortimer, *Edward*, pp. 63–76.

11. *VÆdR* II.11 (pp. 126–7) and Mortimer, 'Edward the Confessor', p. 35.

12. William of Malmesbury, *Gesta Regum Anglorum*, II.196.1, in *William of Malmesbury: Gesta Regum Anglorum / The History of the English Kings*, ed. and trans. R. A. B. Mynors, completed by R. M. Thomson and M. Winterbottom (Oxford: Oxford University Press, 1998), vol. 1, pp. 348–9.

13. For full details, see Mortimer, 'Edward the Confessor', pp. 35–7.

14. E. Williamson, *The Letters of Osbert of Clare, Prior of Westminster* (Oxford: Oxford University Press, 1929), no. 2 (pp. 49–52; at p. 51 for Osbert's comments about the state of Westminster's buildings).

15. P. Chaplais, 'The Original Charters of Herbert and Gervase, Abbots of Westminster, 1121–1157', in *A Medieval Miscellany for Doris Mary Stenton*, ed. P. M. Barnes and C. F. Slade, Pipe Roll Society, New Series, 36 (London: 1962), pp. 89–110.

16. Ibid., p. 95.

17. For the Latin text of this opening of Edward's tomb in 1102, see M. Bloch, 'La Vie de S. Édouard le Confesseur par Osbert de Clare', *Analecta Bollandiana*, 41 (1923), pp. 5–131 (at pp. 121–3); for an English translation, see J. Armitage Robinson, *Gilbert Crispin, Abbot of Westminster: A Study of the Abbey under Norman Rule* (Cambridge: Cambridge University Press, 1911), pp. 24–5. See the account of this occasion in Barlow, *Edward*, pp. 267–9.

18. Barlow, *Edward*, pp. 260–63.

19. E. Mason, 'St Wulfstan's Staff: A Legend and its Uses', *Medium Ævum*, 53 (1984), pp. 157–79, and P. Binski, 'Abbot Berkyng's Tapestries and Matthew Paris's Life of St Edward the Confessor', *Archaeologia*, 109 (1991), pp. 85–100.

20. *VÆdR* I.2 and II.11 (pp. 24–5 and pp. 122–3; and see pp. lxxiii–lxxviii for a discussion by Barlow of the growth and importance of stories concerning Edward's chastity).

21. Williamson, *The Letters of Osbert*, pp. 80–87.

22. Barlow, *Edward*, pp. 274–5.

23. Williamson, *The Letters of Osbert*, no. 19 (pp. 87–8).

24. B. W. Scholz, 'The Canonization of Edward the Confessor', *Speculum*, 26 (1961), pp. 38–60.

25. Barlow, *Edward*, p. 276, and E. Bozoky, 'The Sanctity and Canonisation of Edward the Confessor', in Mortimer, *Edward*, pp. 173–86.

26. The letters are printed in Barlow, *Edward*, Appendix D (pp. 309–24).

27. Barlow, *Edward*, pp. 279–80, and Scholz, 'The Canonization', pp. 51–3.

28. F. M. Powicke (ed. and trans.), *The Life of Ailred of Rievaulx by Walter Daniel* (Oxford: Clarendon Press, 1950), p. 41; and P. Jackson, 'In Translatione Sancti Edwardi Confessoris: The Lost Sermon by Ælred of Rievaulx Found?', *Cistercian Studies Quarterly*, 40 (2005), pp. 45–83.

29. M. L. Dutton (ed.) and J. P. Freeland (trans.), *Aelred of Rievaulx: The Historical Works* (Kalamazoo: Cistercian Publications, 2005), pp. 208–9; and for further

discussion, see Bozoky, 'The Sanctity and Canonisation', pp. 178–84 (particularly pp. 179–80).

30. F. Barlow, 'Becket, Thomas [St Thomas of Canterbury, Thomas of London]', in *ODNB*.

31. Bozoky, 'The Sanctity and Canonisation', p. 182.

32. Binski, *Westminster Abbey*, p. 83.

33. *VÆdR* I.1 (pp. 18–21).

34. British Library, Additional MS 33241.

Further Reading

Frank Barlow's *Edward the Confessor* (New Haven, CT, and London: Yale University Press, 1970; 2nd edn, 1997) is a very engaging and important account of Edward's life, as is the same author's entry on Edward in the *Oxford Dictionary of National Biography*. See also the biography by P. Rex, *King & Saint: The Life of Edward the Confessor* (Stroud: History Press, 2008). A new biography by Tom Licence (*Edward the Confessor: Last of the Royal Blood* (New Haven, CT: 2020)) unfortunately appeared too late for me to take account of it. An extremely useful collection of essays, about many different aspects of Edward's life (and his afterlife), can be found in R. Mortimer (ed.), *Edward the Confessor: The Man and the Legend* (Woodbridge: Boydell & Brewer, 2009). An important account of Edward's time in exile is S. Keynes, 'The Æthelings in Normandy', *Anglo-Norman Studies* (hereafter *ANS*), 13 (1991), pp. 173–205; see also F. Barlow, 'Edward the Confessor's Early Life, Character and Attitudes', *English Historical Review* (hereafter *EHR*), 80 (1965), pp. 225–51, and, for the detail of Edward's actions just before becoming king, J. R. Maddicott, 'Edward the Confessor's Return to England in 1041', *EHR*, 119 (2004), pp. 650–66. For the history of Normandy itself, see D. Bates, *Normandy Before 1066* (London and New York: Longman, 1982), and C. Harper-Bill and E. M. C. van Houts, *A Companion to the Anglo-Norman World* (Woodbridge: Boydell & Brewer, 2003).

A variety of scholarship provides contextual detail for Edward's reign. See, for example, the classic work of F. M. Stenton, *Anglo-Saxon England*, 3rd edn (Oxford: Oxford University Press, 1971). E. John, 'The End of Anglo-Saxon England', in *The Anglo-Saxons*, edited by J. Campbell, E. John and P. Wormald (Oxford: Phaidon

Press, 1982), pp. 214–39, offers a good introduction to the period in general, as does A. Williams, 'England in the Eleventh Century', in *Companion to the Anglo-Norman World*, edited by Harper-Bill and van Houts, pp. 1–18, and N. J. Higham and M. J. Ryan, *The Anglo-Saxon World* (New Haven, CT, and London: Yale University Press, 2013). See further P. Stafford, *Unification and Conquest: A Political and Social History of England in the Tenth and Eleventh Centuries* (London and New York: Arnold, 1989); E. John, *Reassessing Anglo-Saxon England* (Manchester: Manchester University Press, 1996); N. J. Higham, *The Death of Anglo-Saxon England* (Stroud: Sutton Publishing, 1997); and A. Williams, *Kingship and Government in Pre-Conquest England c.500–1066* (Basingstoke: Macmillan Press, 1999). For government in late Anglo-Saxon England, see J. Campbell, *The Anglo-Saxon State* (London: Hambledon and London, 2000); for agents of Anglo-Saxon government, see S. Keynes, 'Regenbald the Chancellor (*sic*)', *ANS*, 10 (1988), pp. 185–222. For the Church in Edward's reign, see F. Barlow, *The English Church, 1000–1066: A Constitutional History* (London: Longman, 1963; 2nd edn, 1979); M. F. Smith, 'The Preferment of Royal Clerks in the Reign of Edward the Confessor', *Haskins Society Journal*, 9 (2001), pp. 159–73; and J. Blair, *The Church in Anglo-Saxon Society* (Oxford: Oxford University Press, 2005). Maps illustrating aspects of Edward's reign can be found in D. Hill, *An Atlas of Anglo-Saxon England* (Oxford: Basil Blackwell, 1981). An extremely useful reference text for the Anglo-Saxon period in general is provided by M. Lapidge et al. (eds), *The Blackwell Encyclopaedia of Anglo-Saxon England* (Oxford: Blackwell Publishers, 1999; 2nd edn, 2014).

Useful discussion of the Norman presence in England before 1066 is provided by M. W. Campbell, 'A Pre-Conquest Norman Occupation of England?', *Speculum*, 46 (1971), pp. 21–30, and by C. P. Lewis, 'The French in England before the Norman Conquest', *ANS*, 17 (1995), pp. 123–41. T. J. Oleson, *The Witenagemot in the Reign of Edward the Confessor* (Oxford: Oxford University Press, 1955), and P. A. Clarke, *The English Nobility Under Edward the Confessor* (Oxford: Clarendon Press, 1994), both provide book-length studies of the king's witan and the nobility in general in Edward's reign. For the dramatic events of 1051–2, see B. Wilkinson, 'Freeman and the Crisis of 1051', *Bulletin of the John Rylands Library*, 22 (1938), pp. 368–87, and M. W. Campbell, 'The Anti-Norman Reaction in England in 1052: Suggested Origins', *Mediaeval Studies*, 38 (1976), pp. 428–41. Much has been written about the question of succession, perhaps particularly D. C. Douglas, 'Edward the Confessor, Duke William of Normandy, and the English Succession', *EHR*, 68 (1953), pp. 526–45; T. J. Oleson, 'Edward the Confessor's Promise of the Throne to Duke William', *EHR*, 72 (1957), pp. 221–8; J. S. Beckerman, 'Succession in Normandy, 1087, and in England, 1066: The Role of Testamentary Custom', *Speculum*, 47 (1972), pp. 258–60; C. Morton, 'Pope Alexander II and the Norman Conquest', *Latomus*, 34 (1975), pp. 362–82; G. Garnett, 'Conquered England, 1066–1215', in *The Oxford Illustrated History of Medieval England*, edited by N. Saul (Oxford: Oxford University Press, 1997), pp. 61–101; and T. Licence, 'Edward the Confessor and the Succession Question: A Fresh Look at the Sources', *ANS*, 39 (2017), pp. 113–28; and see the very useful work on this issue by Stephen Baxter, 'Edward the Confessor and the Succession Question', in Mortimer (ed.), *Edward the Confessor*. For the ways in which Edward's image was constructed, see L. Jones, 'From *Anglorum Basileus* to Norman Saint: The Transformation of Edward the Confessor', *Haskins Society Journal*, 12 (2002), pp. 99–120, and C. E. Karkov, *The Ruler Portraits of Anglo-Saxon England* (Woodbridge: Boydell & Brewer, 2004).

Those wishing to read more about principal actors in Edward's life, his mother (Queen Emma), his wife (Queen Edith) and the leading earl, Godwine, and his sons, in particular Harold, will be able to find numerous interesting scholarly works. On both Emma and Edith, see the crucial book by Pauline Stafford, *Queen Emma & Queen Edith: Queenship and Women's Power in Eleventh-Century*

England (Oxford: Blackwell, 1997). For more about Emma, see F. Barlow, 'Two Notes: Cnut's Second Pilgrimage and Queen Emma's Disgrace in 1043', *EHR*, 73 (1958), pp. 649–56; M. W. Campbell, 'Queen Emma and Ælfgifu of Northampton: Canute the Great's Women', *Mediaeval Scandinavia*, 4 (1971), pp. 66–79; and T. A. Heslop, 'The Production of *de luxe* Manuscripts and the Patronage of King Cnut and Queen Emma', *ASE*, 19 (1990), pp. 151–95. For Edith as queen, see K. E. Cutler, 'Edith, Queen of England, 1045–66', *Mediaeval Studies*, 35 (1973), pp. 222–31. Earl Godwine and his family are deserving of monographs in their own right, and they have received them: F. Barlow, *The Godwins: The Rise and Fall of a Noble Dynasty* (London: Longman, 2002), and E. Mason, *The House of Godwine: The History of a Dynasty* (London and New York: Hambledon and London, 2004). Further detail can be found in M. W. Campbell, 'The Rise of an Anglo-Saxon Kingmaker: Earl Godwine of Wessex', *Canadian Journal of History*, 13 (1978), pp. 17–33; D. G. J. Raraty, 'Earl Godwine of Wessex: The Origins of His Power and his Political Loyalties', *History*, 74 (1989), pp. 3–19; H. R. Loyn, 'Harold, Son of Godwin', in his *Society and Peoples: Studies in the History of England and Wales, c.600–1200* (London: University of London, 1992), pp. 299–321; and G. R. Owen-Crocker (ed.), *King Harold II and the Bayeux Tapestry* (Woodbridge: Boydell & Brewer, 2005). For the comparative wealth of the Godwines and Edward, see R. Fleming, 'Domesday Estates of the King and the Godwines: A Study in Late Saxon Politics', *Speculum*, 58 (1983), pp. 987–1007, and J. Grassi, 'The Lands and Revenues of Edward the Confessor', *EHR*, 117 (2002), pp. 251–83. Entries about all of these individuals can be found in the *Oxford Dictionary of National Biography*.

There are a variety of primary sources that provide details about Edward's life and reign. The *Anglo-Saxon Chronicle* forms one of the most important. The different surviving manuscript copies of the *Anglo-Saxon Chronicle* have different emphases and interests (as discussed in the note in the current volume on p. xv) and so it is important to read across these versions to gain as full a picture as possible of eleventh-century politics. It is most accessible in the translation by D. Whitelock, D. C. Douglas and S. I. Tucker, *The Anglo-Saxon Chronicle: A Revised Translation* (London: Eyre and Spottiswoode, 1961), where one can quickly identify the principal differences between the various manuscript copies. For a recent discussion of the contemporary politics contained in annals 1035–66 in the *Anglo-Saxon Chronicle*, see S. Baxter, 'MS C of the Anglo-Saxon Chronicle and the Politics of Mid-Eleventh-Century England', *EHR*, 122 (2007), pp. 1189–1227, and P. Stafford, 'The Making of Chronicles and the Making of England: The Anglo-Saxon Chronicles after Alfred', *Transactions of the Royal Historical Society*, 27 (2017), pp. 65–86. For the evolution of the *Anglo-Saxon Chronicle*, see S. Keynes, 'Manuscripts of the *Anglo-Saxon Chronicle*', in *The Cambridge History of the Book in Britain*, edited by R. Gameson (Cambridge: Cambridge University Press, 2011), pp. 537–52; and cf. N. P. Brooks, 'Why is the *Anglo-Saxon Chronicle* about Kings?', *ASE*, 39 (2010), pp. 43–70.

Commissioned by Emma, the *Encomium Emmae Reginae* is a text of enormous significance and interest, which provides views about the early stages of Edward's life. A text and translation with an important introduction that gives much contextual information is A. Campbell (ed. and trans.) and S. Keynes (supplementary introduction), *Encomium Emmae Reginae*, Camden Classic Reprints 4 (Cambridge: Cambridge University Press, 1998); for discussion of a new ending to the text only recently found, see S. Keynes and R. Love, 'Earl Godwine's Ship', *ASE*, 38 (2009), pp. 185–223. For a Norman text of the mid eleventh century giving details about Edward, see E. M. C. van Houts, 'Historiography and Hagiography at Saint-Wandrille: The "Inventio et Miracula Sancti Vulfranni"', *ANS*, 12 (1989), pp. 233–51.

The *Vita Ædwardi Regis* constitutes another critical source for Edward's reign. The Latin text (which is partly prosimetrical, i.e.

combines passages of prose and verse) and a translation can be found in F. Barlow (ed. and trans.), *The Life of King Edward the Confessor Who Rests at Westminster* (Oxford: Oxford University Press, 1962; 2nd edn, 1992). The writing of the *Vita* was commissioned by Edith, wife of Edward, and daughter of Earl Godwine, and this fact colours much of what is said in the text itself. Much has been written about the thematic unity of the *Vita*, its purpose, its authorship and its date of composition. The *Vita* was traditionally attributed to an anonymous writer and that is how it is referred to in this book; recent scholarship has argued in favour of Folcard being the author, a Flemish hagiographer who wrote a variety of saints' *vitae*; see T. Licence, 'The Date and Authorship of the *Vita Ædwardi regis*', *ASE*, 44 (2015), pp. 259–85. For an important recent analysis of the text, particularly its handling of the Godwine family, see E. M. Tyler, *England in Europe: English Royal Women and Literary Patronage, c.1000–c.1150* (Toronto: University of Toronto Press, 2017), pp. 135–201. For extra passages in the *Vita Ædwardi* recently discovered among the papers of Tudor and Jacobean antiquaries, see H. Summerson, 'Tudor Antiquaries and the *Vita Ædwardi Regis*', *ASE*, 38 (2009), pp. 157–84.

The documentary records for Edward's reign comprise royal diplomas and writs. Diplomas are catalogued in P. H. Sawyer, *Anglo-Saxon Charters: An Annotated List and Bibliography* (London: Royal Historical Society, 1968), where each diploma is given a so-called 'S' number. Diplomas are individually edited and provided with commentaries according to the archive in which they are preserved; these modern editions can be found in the British Academy 'Anglo-Saxon Charters' series, published by Oxford University Press under the auspices of the Royal Historical Society https://www.thebritishacademy. ac.uk/anglo-saxon-charters. An online catalogue with much useful bibliographical and explanatory material can be found here: https:// esawyer.lib.cam.ac.uk/about/index.html. A healthy collection of writs survives from Edward's reign, all of which are edited, translated and discussed in F. E. Harmer, *Anglo-Saxon Writs* (Manchester: Manchester University Press, 1952).

Two Norman authors, William of Jumièges and William of Poitiers, who were writing in the early to mid 1070s, produced texts that offer a Norman perspective on many important eleventh-century political events. Their works can be found in their original Latin with accompanying translation in E. M. C. van Houts (ed. and trans.), *The Gesta Normannorum Ducum of William of Jumièges, Orderic Vitalis, and Robert of Torigni*, 2 vols (Oxford: Oxford University Press, 1992–5), and R. H. C. Davis and M. Chibnall (eds and trans.), *The Gesta Guillelmi of William of Poitiers* (Oxford: Oxford University Press, 1998). Given their Norman bias, some of the views in these works are quite different to those found in English sources and are therefore crucial when attempting to reconstruct political history of the pre-1066 period.

Texts composed by Anglo-Norman historians, from the late eleventh century to the mid twelfth century, constitute sources of vital importance, both as near-contemporary witnesses to events from Edward's lifetime (albeit with their own bias and purpose) and as repositories of information not found elsewhere. Of particular importance for Edward's reign are works by William of Malmesbury and John of Worcester: R. A. B. Mynors, R. M. Thomson and M. Winterbottom (eds and trans.), *William of Malmesbury: Gesta Regum Anglorum / The History of the English Kings*, 2 vols (Oxford: Oxford University Press, 1998–9); M. Winterbottom and R. M. Thomson (eds and trans.), *William of Malmesbury: Gesta Pontificum Anglorum / The History of the English Bishops*, 2 vols (Oxford: Oxford University Press, 1998–2002); R. R. Darlington and P. McGurk (eds), J. Bray and P. McGurk (trans.), *The Chronicle of John of Worcester*, vol. 2: *The Annals from 450 to 1066* (Oxford: Oxford University Press, 1995); and P. McGurk (ed. and trans.), *The Chronicle of John of Worcester*, vol. 3: *The Annals from 1067 to 1140* (Oxford: Oxford University Press, 1998).

In addition to the textual record, one should not neglect the material sources that bear directly on events in Edward's lifetime. The Bayeux Tapestry is the most famous example. It is nothing short of a miracle that this extremely fragile artefact has survived from the late eleventh century to the present day. It was once put on display by Napoleon as an object designed to inspire French national pride and later survived an order by a Nazi official for German soldiers to take it with them when retreating from France. Carola Hicks's *The Bayeux Tapestry: The Life Story of a Masterpiece* (London: Vintage Books, 2007) provides fascinating details about its later history. For the Tapestry itself, see F. Stenton (ed.), *The Bayeux Tapestry: A Comprehensive Survey*, 2nd edn (London: Phaidon Press, 1965); a complete facsimile can be found in D. M. Wilson, *The Bayeux Tapestry* (London: Thames and Hudson, 1985). There has been much debate about the origins of the Tapestry and the meaning(s) of many of its scenes. Edward features in some of the most memorable parts of the Tapestry. For an introduction to some of these issues, see N. P. Brooks and H. E. Walker, 'The Authority and Interpretation of the Bayeux Tapestry', *ANS*, 1 (1978), pp. 1–34 (and pp. 191–9 for associated notes). For an important collection of essays about the Tapestry, see R. Gameson (ed.), *The Study of the Bayeux Tapestry* (Woodbridge: Boydell & Brewer, 1997). Coins also form important evidence for Edward's reign, in terms of their designs (which can tell us a great deal about royal aspirations), their inscriptions and their weight/fineness. For a very useful overview of Edward's coinage, with references to much recent literature, see R. Naismith, *Medieval European Coinage, with a Catalogue of the Coins in the Fitzwilliam Museum, Cambridge*, vol. 8: *Britain and Ireland c.400–1066* (Cambridge: Cambridge University Press, 2017), pp. 271–6. For a recent survey of the history of Westminster Abbey, see D. Cannadine (ed.), *Westminster Abbey: A Church in History* (New Haven, CT, and London: Yale University Press, 2019).

The development of Edward's image, status and cult following his death is treated in great detail in Barlow's *Edward the Confessor*. See also B. W. Scholz, 'The Canonization of Edward the Confessor', *Speculum*, 26 (1961), pp. 38–60; B. R. O'Brien, *God's Peace and King's Peace: The Laws of Edward the Confessor* (Philadelphia: University of Pennsylvania Press, 1999); R. Mortimer, 'Edward the Confessor: The Man and the Legend', in Mortimer (ed.), *Edward the Confessor*, pp. 1–40, and, in the same edited volume, E. Bozoky, 'The Sanctity and Canonisation of Edward the Confessor', pp. 173–86. For the cult of Edward in the thirteenth century, see P. Binski, *Westminster Abbey and the Plantagenets: Kingship and the Presentation of Power 1200–1400* (New Haven, CT, and London: Yale University Press, 1995), and D. A. Carpenter, 'King Henry III and St Edward the Confessor: The Origins of the Cult', *EHR*, 122 (2007), pp. 865–91. For Osbert of Clare, see M. Bloch, 'La Vie de S. Édouard le Confesseur par Osbert de Clare', *Analecta Bollandiana*, 41 (1923), pp. 5–131, and E. Williamson, *The Letters of Osbert of Clare, Prior of Westminster* (Oxford: Oxford University Press, 1929; reprinted 1998). For Ailred of Rievaulx, see F. M. Powicke (ed. and trans.), *The Life of Ailred of Rievaulx by Walter Daniel* (Oxford: Clarendon Press, 1950; reprinted 1978), and F. Marzella (ed.), *Aelredi Rievallensis, Vita Sancti Ædwardi Regis et Confessoris*, Corpus Christianorum Continuatio Mediaevalis IIIA, Aelredi Rievallensis Opera Omnia 7, Opera Historica et Hagiographica (Turnhout: Brepols Publishers, 2017).

Picture Credits

1. An example of Edward the Confessor's 'Pacx' type of coinage (Classical Numismatic Group, LLC: https://www.cngcoins.com)
2. An example of Edward the Confessor's 'Pointed Helmet' type of coinage (Classical Numismatic Group, LLC: https://www.cngcoins.com)
3. An example of Edward the Confessor's 'Sovereign/Eagles' type of coinage (Classical Numismatic Group, LLC: https://www.cngcoins.com)
4. A single-sheet diploma of Edward the Confessor, granting land to a certain Leofric, his chaplain (reproduced by kind permission of the Dean and Chapter of Exeter Cathedral; catalogued in P. H. Sawyer, *Anglo-Saxon Charters: An Annotated List and Bibliography* (London: Royal Historical Society, 1968), no. 1003)
5. A charter of Duke Robert I of Normandy for the abbey of Fécamp. Musée de la Bénédictine de Fécamp, no. 7 (published by kind permission of Palais Bénédictine, Fécamp, France)
6. A later addition made to folio 100v of the manuscript containing the text known as the *Historia Regum*. Cambridge, Corpus Christi College, 139 (The Parker Library, Corpus Christi College, Cambridge)
7. An original writ of Edward the Confessor for Archbishop Stigand and the community of Christ Church, Canterbury (© The British Library Board. All Rights Reserved/ Bridgeman Images; catalogued in Sawyer, *Anglo-Saxon Charters*, no. 1088)
8. The depiction of Edward the Confessor's death in the Bayeux Tapestry (detail of the Bayeux Tapestry – 11th Century, with special permission from the City of Bayeux)
9. Westminster Abbey in the Bayeux Tapestry (detail of the Bayeux Tapestry – 11th Century, with special permission from the City of Bayeux)
10. Edward the Confessor's shrine in Westminster Abbey (© The Dean and Chapter of Westminster Abbey)
11. Image from a manuscript containing a copy of the *Encomium Emmae Reginae*. British Library, Additional MS 33241 (© The British Library Board. All Rights Reserved/Bridgeman Images)

Acknowledgements

In writing this book I have relied on the published work of many scholars; as far as possible this has been indicated in the Notes and Further Reading, but the constraints of space have meant that the citing of scholarship has been limited to essential reading. I am most grateful to Professor Tom Licence, Dr Richard Mortimer, Dr Rory Naismith and Dr Levi Roach, all of whom very kindly read and commented on the entirety of the book and improved it in numerous ways. The opinions expressed here are my own and any errors that remain are my responsibility. I would also like to thank Stuart Proffitt and Kate Parker at Penguin for their careful reading of my text and making it better. The idea for the book was born during a period of sabbatical leave at Harvard University with my partner, Sasha Haco. Had it not been for her unfailing support and encouragement, the idea would never have reached fruition. The book is dedicated to her.

Index